RATIONAL MARKET ECONOMICS

A Compass for the Beginning Investor

Bernie Keating

authorHOUSE®

AuthorHouse™
1663 Liberty Drive
Bloomington, IN 47403
www.authorhouse.com
Phone: 1-800-839-8640

First published by AuthorHouse   5/25/2011

ISBN: 978-1-4634-0163-4 (sc)
ISBN: 978-1-4634-0162-7 (hc)
ISBN: 978-1-4634-0161-0 (e)

Library of Congress Control Number: 2011908328

Printed in the United States of America

Any people depicted in stock imagery provided by Thinkstock are models,
and such images are being used for illustrative purposes only.
Certain stock imagery © Thinkstock.

This book is printed on acid-free paper.

Because of the dynamic nature of the Internet, any web addresses or links contained in
this book may have changed since publication and may no longer be valid. The views
expressed in this work are solely those of the author and do not necessarily reflect the
views of the publisher, and the publisher hereby disclaims any responsibility for them.

CONTENTS

PREFACE

If you utilize others for assistance with your investments, you will want to understand and concur -- or dissent -- with their advice. This book will provide some of the knowledge needed. We are not stock market experts, but we do need some investing savvy.

During a long career in a multi-national corporation, I had a 401(k). Then I retired, took a lump-sum pension package, rolled it and my 401(k) into an IRA, and I was in charge of my own financial future. Talk about "white knuckle" time.

I suddenly faced the challenge of investments; so I went back to school. Struggling through the financial pages and attending investment seminars, I gradually digested the complexities of GDP, prime rate, leading indicators, and all the jargon of the trade. Afloat in a sea of statistics with a new tide arriving each day, I began to identify the basics; I could reach in to extract what was important in the financial news. This was a major breakthrough.

I began to organize what I had learned about the economy and investment. This became a self-discovery process and motivation for writing a book. I wrote it for myself; that was twenty years ago. Since then my net worth has doubled -- testimony to success. Now I am up-dating the book. You are invited to accompany me on this journey, and if it becomes a discovery process for you also, I shall be twice blessed.

ONE:
WHY ECONOMICS?

Some knowledge of economics is necessary. Investing is a skirmish fought on the battlefield of the economy; so we need to look at the arena where it is fought. Economics is a Greek word relating to "management of a household," and it starts in the gut of the individual with how people react to the events in their lives. This notion did not exist several centuries ago before people had "connected the dots," and realized how things in their lives – the needs and resources --were interrelated.

An Englishman, Adam Smith, became the first economist when he published ***An Inquiry into the Nature and Causes of the Wealth of Nations*** in 1776, the same year that Thomas Jefferson wrote our Declaration of Independence. [1] No one had realized until then how the fragments of social activity fit together in a cohesive whole. Smith accomplished that and the result was a blueprint for a new social science called economics, which analyzes the products, distribution, and consumption of goods and services. It explains how things interact throughout society not only in business, finance, and government; but also in crime, education, the family, health, law, politics, religion, social institutions, war, and science.

Economics is generally dealt with on two levels: macroeconomics and microeconomics. Macroeconomics looks at the big picture and deals with the performance, structure, behavior and decision-making of the entire economy. Microeconomics comes from the Greek word meaning "small," and focuses on the details. It looks at the allocation of limited resources in markets where goods or services are being bought or sold. The reason we look at both macro -- and micro -- economics is because these will

1

have considerable impact on how our investments will fare in the stock market.

There are two opposing philosophies of how much control should be maintained over the economy: Free Market, and Keynesian.

Free Market relies on minimal economic intervention and regulation by the state, except to enforce private contracts and the ownership of property. Keynesian advocates monetary policies by the central bank and fiscal policies by the government to stabilize the business cycle. [2] While these two opposing philosophies may seem somewhat academic, we realized during the 2007 financial meltdown their differences can create great impact in the economy and in the stock market.

One of the yardsticks used to measure the economy is the Gross Domestic Product (GDP). It is the market value of all goods and services produced within a country in a given period of time. All countries like to maintain their GDP in a positive direction. The United States administrations have a goal to maintain it stabilized within the 2% to 4% annual growth rate. When the GDP growth rate is below zero for two consecutive quarters, an economy is considered to be in recession. It seldom climbs above the 5% annual growth rate in the United States, but the GDP of a number of emerging foreign countries such as China often climb up to a 10% annual growth rate because they have started from a lower base.

Economies are seldom entirely stable but fluctuate over several months or years, involving shifts between periods of relatively rapid growth (expansion or boom) and periods of relative stagnation or decline (contraction or recession). These are referred to as the business cycles. A successful investor should understand the things that cause the instability.

An investor must understand what is going on in the economy. If the economic parameters are weak, how will that affect their investments, or what if the economy is booming? Is this the time to buy, sell or hold their cards close to the vest? As in all professional disciplines, an investor must learn the basics of the trade.

TWO:
PARAMETERS OF THE ECONOMY

The economy is a complex social phenomenon with many dimensions, and some of these measure important parameters of the stock market. These are:

> Corporate Earnings
> Interest Rates
> Inflation
> Liquidity
> $ Exchange rate

An investor who keeps focus on these economic parameters will be in a better position to predict the future course of the market, or at least be able to react more intelligently to events as they arise. There are also many secondary factors that affect the market, but they do this mostly through the influence that they exert on these primary parameters. Here is an overview:

CORPORATE EARNINGS: Investors buy stock to gain part ownership of a corporation so they can share in its earnings, or in growth that will lead to future earnings. The price they are willing to pay for stock is based on current earnings and their perception of future earnings, compared to what they could make from other investments.

INTEREST RATES: Interest rates and the stock market have a tendency to move in opposite directions because of two reasons:

1. Interest bearing investments are competitors of equity stocks for available investor's dollars.
2. Interest rates are used by the Federal Reserve as a tool to fuel or to retard the economic growth rate, and this has a major impact on corporate earnings.

The net effect is that the stock market normally reacts to changes in interest rates faster and more sharply than most other factors.

Which of these interest rates are the most important to watch: prime rate set by commercial banks, discount rate or federal funds rate set by the Federal Reserve, or T bill rates determined by bids in the open market? Also, how does the Federal Reserve Bank go about the control of interest rates?

INFLATION: The Federal Reserve considers inflation one of the greatest threats to our economy; so they place high priority on its control. One of the tools they use is interest rates. As inflation increases, interest rates are raised by the Federal Reserve as a means to cause inflation to be decreased.

LIQUIDITY: Liquidity means how much money supply and other liquid assets exist that are readily available to the economy. It involves both how much is available and how fluid it is to flow into various investments. When liquidity is too low, the economy and the stock market suffer. When liquidity is high and investor's pockets are full of money, they tend to buy stock; so the markets often rise.

U.S.DOLLAR EXCHANGE RATE: Until recent years it made little difference to the investor how much a U. S. dollar was worth compared to the Euro or other foreign currencies. That has changed in recent decades because we now deal with a global economy. How important is exchange rate to the U. S. Stock Market? In the view of Federal Reserve Chief Paul Volcker, exchange rate adjustments were a major contributing cause to the sudden market crash that occurred in October 1987.

These five primary economic parameters are interrelated. As one of them goes up or down it may cause another parameter to move in parallel or in the opposite direction. For example: if the Federal Reserve issued new currency to buy back government bonds, which could fuel a rise in inflation; then to head-off this rise, the Federal Reserve may increase the federal funds interest rate, which would have the effect of bringing inflation back down again. Seldom are all five parameters stable or in lock step.

SOME ECONOMIC AND MARKET LANGUAGE:

It is difficult to discuss the stock market without using common jargon. Some of this provides benchmarks to relate today's market for comparison with other time periods, other U.S. stock market indices, or with other indices in the global market. Let's review some of the terms the investor will encounter:

S&P 500 INDEX: One of the principle benchmarks for the U.S. Stock Market is the S&P 500 Index. This Index is a composite based on the value of the 500 largest corporations in America. These corporations contain 70% of the U.S. equity market's value and capture 60% of the daily trading volume; so it has a close correlation with the broad stock market, and is normally the most representative of the overall market trend.

The S&P 500 Index is based on Return on Investment (ROI), a measure of profit that is discussed later. The change in this Index over a period of time reflects not only the change in stock price, which is the capital gain, but also the dividends that are paid during the period; therefore, the change in the S & P 500 Index represents the Return on Investment for this large segment of the stock market. For example; if the price of stock increased by 7% during the year and there was a 3% increase in value due to dividends, then the S&P 500 Index increased in value by 10%, and we could hazard a guess that the U.S. Stock Market had a total return on investment of about 10%.

OTHER STOCK MARKET INDICES: There are other indexes in common usage. The Dow Jones Industrial Average is based on 30 large corporations that have been chosen by the Dow Jones Company, the former owner of the Wall Street Journal. The NASDAQ Index is based on a cross section of small companies whose stock is sold over-the-counter as identified by the National Association of Securities Dealers.

RETURN ON INVESTMENT (ROI): Return on Investment (ROI) is the total earning the investor receives for his stock, which includes capital gain (or loss) plus dividends and interest. For example; if you invest $10,000 in a thousand shares of stock at $10/share; and in one year it has increased in value by $2,000 dollars to $12/share and it paid a dividend

5

of $1,000, your Return on Investment is $3,000, or 30%. The ROI is the bottom line that most investors are interested in.

YIELD: is the earnings produced, but normally does not factor in the capital gains. In the above example, the investor receives a $1,000 dividend, which is the yield. What is the point of ignoring the capital gain and using the term yield? Many investors are primarily interested in the dividends that come from a fixed capital investment and are not in the business of trading stock. For debt instruments such as Treasury Notes, Bonds, and Money Market the two terms, ROI and yield, become interchangeable; here the annual yield produced in the form of interest is the same as the ROI. Because these terms are commonly misused, you can never be certain what is meant until you do the calculation yourself.

PRICE TO EARNINGS RATIO (P/E): An important number investors look at is the ratio between the price of a stock and its earnings, expressed as the Price/Earnings ratio (P/E). Many investors look at this number for an individual company to decide if the earnings adequately reflect support for the price of a share of that company's stock, while other investors look at the number for the S&P 500 Index to gage the earnings for the overall market. The earnings are normally based on the earnings of the past year, but sometimes other time periods are substituted such as the projected earnings for the forecasted next year, so using the number calls for some investigation.

The average P/E for the S&P 500 Index over the past 50 years was 15.5. This means that the price paid for an average share of stock in an S&P 500 Index fund was 15.5 times its earning over the past year.

SUMMARY:

The five principle parameters of the economy that affect the stock market are:

> Corporate earnings
> Interest Rates
> Inflation
> Liquidity
> $ Exchange rate

An investor need to become familiar with common stock market terms, such as:

S&P 500 Index: a principle measure of the U.S. Stock Market.

Other stock indices: Dow Jones Industrial Average and NASDAQ

(ROI) Rate of Return: total earnings from investment in stock.

Yield: earnings that exclude capital gains.

(P/E) Price Earnings Ratio: the ratio of the price of stock with earnings for the past year.

THREE:
WHERE DO WE START?

While there are many kinds of investments, I will narrow my focus to the ownership of equity (corporate stock) that is bought and sold on the U.S. Stock Exchange. A purchase of equity could be accomplished as simply as a buyer handing cash to secure a purchase and the seller handing over the stock certificate, but today it is normally accomplished on a stock exchange. Our American Stock Exchange started a couple hundred years ago under a tree in New York City where men engaged in a bartering process. The tree has since been replaced by the New York Stock Exchange on Wall Street and it may eventually be replaced by computers using the internet or other modern alternatives. The bartering process has always been a dog-eat-dog operation -- read Shakespeare's *Merchant of Venice* for a look at the market of six hundred years ago on the Rialto Bridge in Venice when Shylock wanted his pound of flesh for an unpaid debt.

Every person offering something for sale is looking for someone who wants to buy. They are each trying to out-do the other, and it remains the same process today even though it may have become impersonal and more complex. Since its earliest beginnings, the stock market has struggled with borderline corruption, insider information, minimal regulations, what information is ethical to share with whom, and how these things can be controlled. Additionally, all investments are subject to the jeopardy of risk compared with reward or potential return. A higher potential return normally is the result of assuming a greater risk. These problems cannot be totally eliminated; so that presents additional peril for a naive investor. Buyer beware!

We must always remember that the stock market is a bartering process where every transaction involves a buyer and a seller who each act on the basis of their own self-serving needs. We must remind ourselves of this when we begin to think the market is based on logic or some scientific laws. Perhaps one scientific principle I could cite as a former physicist is that the stock market is always in a state of unstable equilibrium. One of the roles of a "specialist" on the floor of the New York Stock Exchange is to "create a market," thereby establishing non-equilibrium to stimulate the bartering process.

When I was an executive in Owens-Illinois Inc. with good information about the future of my own company, I invested in its stock. After I retired, I was no longer comfortable with what little information I still had about company performance; so I stopped investing in the company. Gradually I learned that I do not have sufficient access to information about any company to gamble a substantial part of my portfolio on one. But I do have some degree of expertise and information about the overall Stock Market; so my equity investments today are almost entirely with an Index Fund.

In the following five chapters, we will take a closer look at each of the primary parameters of the economy that affect the stock market.

FOUR:
CORPORATE EARNINGS

Investors buy stock because they want the corporate earnings plus any growth in the value of the stock. My own investment focus is on the broad stock market; so instead of buying stock in individual companies, I buy shares in an S&P 500 Index fund that is a composite of the 500 largest companies.

Chart # 1 gives a graph of the index for the past several decades together with the earnings per share (adjusted 10 times so they fit on the same chart). The chart provides a picture of the relationship between corporate earnings and the S&P 500 Index.

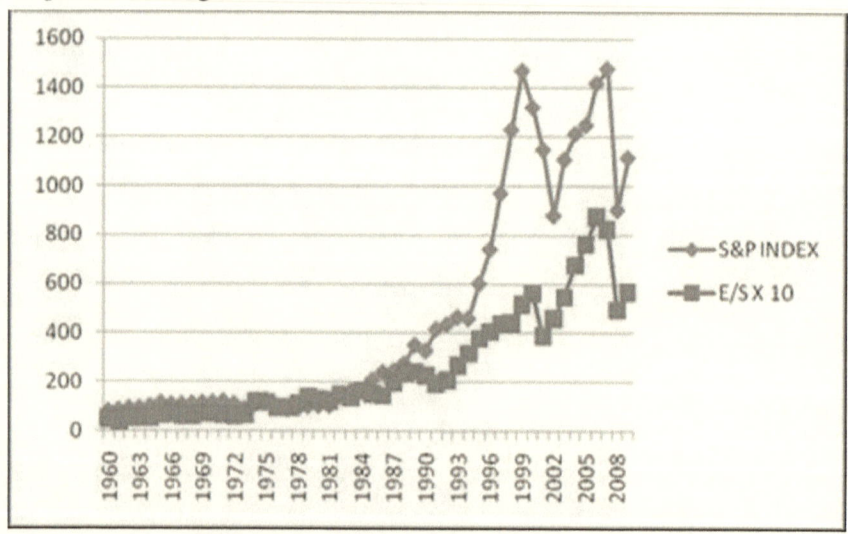

Chart #1. S&P 500 INDEX AND CORPORATE EARNINGS *
* Annual Earnings per share x 10

As seen on the chart, the Index was relatively flat for several decades as a result of poor corporate earnings. Then in about 1985 the earnings began to improve, which led to a climb in the blue line of the Index. In fact, the Index rose at a faster rate than supported by the increase in earnings as the result of investors speculating on future earnings. Another factor, the Price/Earnings ratio (discussed in the endnotes), now comes into play in determining the price of stock. [3]

The Index continued to rise for several years and then in 2001 it fell dramatically to 815 in the aftermath of the Twin Tower disaster in New York City. Regaining its growth, it rose to a new high in 2007. This rapid gain was highly speculative and based on anticipation of vastly improved earnings in the period ahead. The corporate earnings reached a high in late 2007, but dropped to a loss by the end of 2008 as a result of the Financial Meltdown. The S&P Index lost nearly 50% of its value in the aftermath. Then as corporate earnings began to recover, the Index began to again move upward in a new bull market.

The chart shows there is not an exact correlation between a rise in corporate earnings and the index; they do not move up or down in lock-step. This is because the psychology of the investors may perceive a change in earnings as having a greater or lesser impact on the price they are willing to pay for stock. For example, when investors see good times ahead and are bullish, they may become speculative and pay an increasing increment for stock. This relationship between earnings and the price of stock is expressed as the Price/Earnings ratio (P/E). The ratio is a number that has meaning only in a historical context. Over the last 50 years, it has averaged 15.5. When the ratio falls lower than this, it suggests investors are bearish and are being cautious, and it seldom goes as low as 10, even in hard times. When the ratio moves above its average, it is an indication investors are bullish and are willing to pay an additional increment for stock. Whenever it reaches 20, beware, because the stock market has moved up into a speculative range. During the past decade, the P/E was often above 20, suggesting a highly speculative market. It was at 29.6 before the Twin Tower disaster of 9/11, and we know what happened to that market.

The message to take from this chapter is that investors buy stock for the corporate earnings they will receive or an increase in the future value of the stock; and a good gauge they often utilize is the Price/Earnings ratio that reflects the psychology of investors at any given time.

FIVE:
INFLATION

Investors do not buy or sell stock solely on the basis of corporate earnings; they look at other things that will have a major influence on the future course of the market. Inflation is by far the most important of these basic market parameters. Why the paranoia about inflation? Well, for one thing, it is a major factor that causes the stock market to go up or down: <u>inflation and the market move in opposite directions.</u> When inflation is increasing, the stock market drops. When inflation is low, the market will be stable or rise if other factors are also positive. Chart #2 shows the historical relationship between inflation and the S&P 500 Index, and suggests they move opposite to each other.

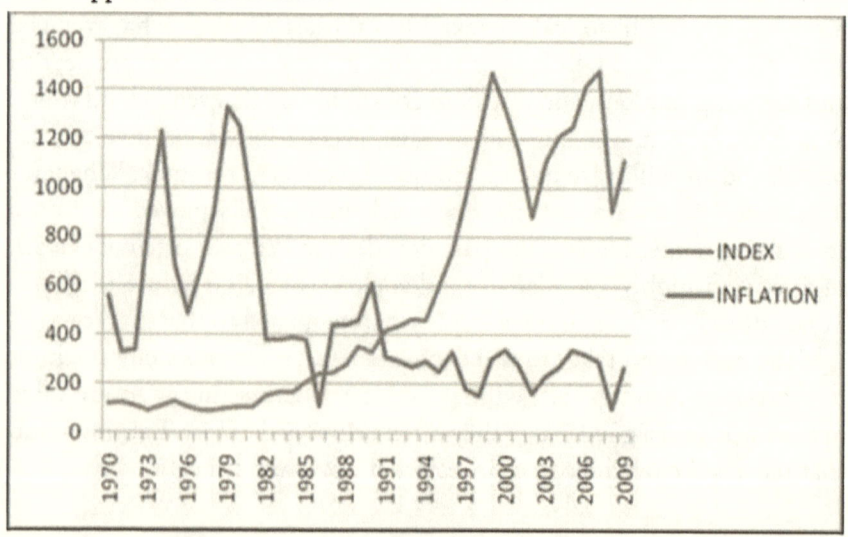

Chart #2 S& P 500 INDEX AND INFLATION

This forty year inflation profile begins in 1969 when inflation was increased by the Vietnam War, which we were not willing to pay for with taxes. That was followed by two oil shocks in 1973 and 1978 that dramatically raised the cost of living. By the end of 1979, inflation in the U.S. economy had reached 13.3%. This high inflation was ultimately conquered by the Federal Reserve in 1982 under the leadership of Paul Volker, Chairman of the Federal Reserve, using a tight money supply policy that ultimately caused interest rates to reach 19%. He simply clamped down on the money supply until there was no liquidity in the system to fuel inflation.

The effect of inflation on the stock market during these four decades was sometimes dramatic. The market languished in relative inactivity during the 60's because of poor corporate earnings; and then the Vietnam War and oil shocks caused high inflation through the 70's, which depressed stock prices. In 1982, after inflation had been conquered, the market took off on a bull market run with the S&P 500 Index climbing to 1469 in 1999. After a drop in 2001 due to the Twin Tower disaster, it climbed again to 1478 in 2007. That growth during the 90's would have started decades earlier if it were not for the financial shocks that caused the high inflation of the early 1970's.

WHAT IS INFLATION?

Now that we have seen some effects of inflation, let's look at what it is and why it has such a strong effect on the economy and the stock market. Inflation is the erosion in the purchasing power of money.

If the government suddenly printed and circulated five percent more dollars, then five percent more dollars would be chasing the same amount of goods and services; so their prices would gradually increase five percent. This would not happen because the goods and services were of greater value, but because the currency had lost five percent of its purchasing power. That is five percent inflation.

Using the same sort of illustration, inflation can be caused in another way. If the government does not change the amount of money in circulation, but the oil producing OPEC countries suddenly raise the cost of oil so that the same amount of goods and services now cost us more, then our dollar again has lost part of its purchasing power.

The culprit does not have to be a foreign element such as OPEC. If Detroit continues to produce the same number of autos, using the same amount of manpower, materials, and productivity, but raises the price it is charging, then our goods and services now cost us more, and our dollar has again lost part of its purchasing power. <u>Wage increases that are not matched by an equivalent improvement in productivity add to inflation.</u>

HOW IS INFLATION MEASURED ?

The U.S. Labor Department measures the rate of inflation and reports it monthly. It calculates what is called the Consumer Price Index, which is the official U.S. measure of inflation. It is calculated using a weighted cross-section of goods and services, called the "bread basket," that consumer's use, which includes the cost for such things as:

Fuel
Auto and transportation
Home purchase, rental, and maintenance
Food in a typical food basket
Clothing
Entertainment
Education and many other things

Each month the Labor Department goes into the marketplace to determine the price of a composite of these items and calculates the overall cost of living for the typical person. This existing "bread basket" method for calculating the amount of inflation has been challenged. A federal commission in 1996 who were exploring the subject came to the conclusion that the bread basket was no longer typical of consumers' buying habits and was over-stating inflation.

For example, while the bread basket measured the price of goods and services as purchased in traditional retail stores, in actual fact the consumers had shifted a substantial part of their buying to discount stores where prices were lower. They were also substituting less costly items to replace those included in the basket. In many other related purchasing activities, consumers found a way to circumvent the higher prices of the bread basket the U.S. Labor Department used as a benchmark to measure inflation. In early 1997 in testifying before Congress, Chairman Greenspan agreed with the findings of the commission, and he stated that current inflation rates were over-stated by 1%. This is a very substantial measurement error. He urged congress to take action to correct the method of measuring inflation. As a consequence, the basic measurement of inflation has gradually changed over the years, and there are various other definitions such as "core inflation," that include or exclude certain segments of the economy.

SUMMARY:

Inflation is important to the financial markets for two reasons: a rising inflation rate usually triggers an increase by the Federal Reserve in interest rates, which will cause the market to drop; and a high inflation impacts on the business cycle, which often brings economic expansion to a halt.

All governments consider inflation one of the major threats to the economic stability of their country. Governments attempt to follow monetary fiscal policies that will keep inflation in check. Their policies utilize interest rates, money supply, and other means to achieve this stability. The financial markets are the beneficiary of these policies when they are successful, but if they fail, the markets suffer a downturn in the economy, which is caught-up in the grip of run-away inflation.

SIX:
INTEREST RATES

The subject of interest is a tough challenge to get our arms around and simplify, because interest enters into financial transactions under so many different forms and names. Let's try to sort through this complex subject.

The prevailing rate of interest in the economy at any given time has a major impact on financial markets, and it is a causative factor that moves the stock market up or down. Interest rates and the stock market have a tendency to move in opposite directions. When the interest rates go up, the stock market goes down, and vice versa. There are two reasons for this: interest rates and the stock market compete for the same investor dollars, and high interest rates have a negative impact on the economy.

Interest rates and the stock market compete for the same investors' dollars because the investor can buy equity stock that gives him ownership in a corporation, or the same dollars can be invested in interest bearing instruments, such as treasury bills, certificates of deposit or money market funds. These latter are called debt instruments, because someone else is going into debt to the investor. Real estate and bonds are other competitive investment options. When interest rates fall and debt instruments become unattractive, the stock market normally moves upward as investors move their dollars into equity stock for its higher return. Conversely when interest rates rise, investors move back into these interest bearing investments and the stock market falls.

The second reason that interest rates and the stock market move opposite each other is that high interest rates have a negative impact on the economy. In its control of monetary policy, the Federal Reserve uses interest rate adjustments as a means to heat up or to cool down the economy. When it is heating up too rapidly and the Fed fears that inflation will increase, they raise interest rates as a means to slow things down. Investors then know that corporate earnings will suffer; so they move out of stock into the more attractive debt instruments.

Conversely when the economy needs a shot in the arm, the Federal Reserve reduces interest rates and this normally has the effect of improving corporate earnings; so investors buy stock. The net effect of these two things (competition and impact on the economy) is why the stock market normally reacts to changes of interest rates faster and more sharply than other factors.

The following chart #3 shows the relationship between the 3 month Treasury bill interest rate and the S&P 500 Index. They are near opposites of each other, and when one rises, the other falls. The chart used the 3 month Treasury bill as representative of the rate of interest. These Treasury bills are sold by the government at auction in the open market; so they represent what investors are willing to pay for short term, debt type investments at any given time.

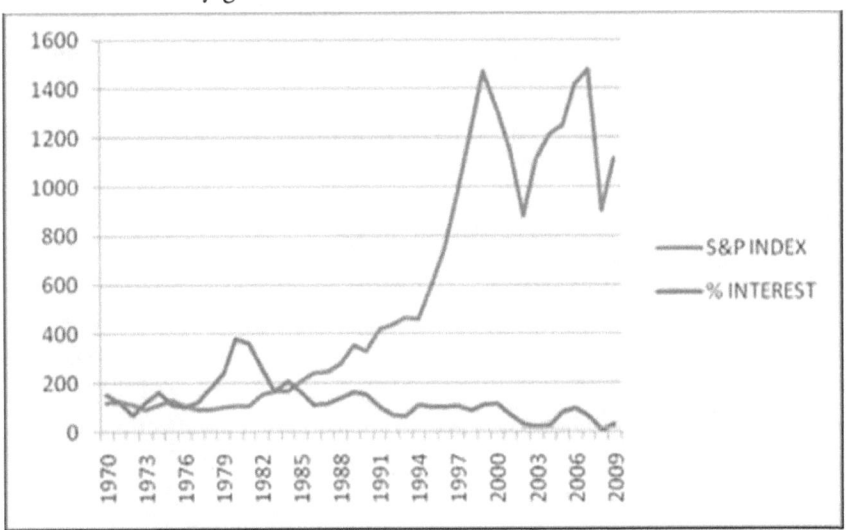

CHART #3 S&P 500 INDEX AND % INTEREST

DESCRIPTION OF INTEREST RATES:

A finger walk through the financial pages will expose you to many different kinds of interest, so let's sort them out.

<u>Interest</u>: The price paid for the use of money.

<u>Simple interest</u>: The amount of interest earned in a given unit of time that is normally one year. The term is seldom used.

<u>Effective rate of interest</u>: The actual rate of interest earned in one year. An investment of $100 that pays an effective rate of 6% will earn you $6.00 in one year's time.

<u>Compound interest</u>: The interest earned in each time period is added to the principal amount, so the potential for earnings keeps compounding because the kitty is growing larger.

<u>Nominal rate of interest</u>. This is a compounded interest rate which will specify the time period during which the rate is compounded.

INTEREST CATEGORIES:

Now, with these basics in mind, let's look at some of the interest rates bankers deal with. Interest rates can be categorized by type of investment:

* Rates directly controlled by the Federal Reserve.
* Government borrowing by competitive bid in the open market.
* Loans made by commercial banks.
* Monetary deposits by investors in banks.

INTEREST RATES CONTROLLED BY THE FEDERAL RESERVE

<u>Discount rate</u>: The rate of interest that the Federal Reserve charges for the reserve money they loan to their member banks is at the top of the interest hierarchy. This money flows downhill in commercial loans and increases the nation's money supply. In a trickle down process, this is at the top of the hill.

<u>Federal Funds rate</u>: The interest rate that commercial banks charge one another for short term loans. The Federal Reserve also uses this as a means of monetary control and can largely determine the rate by buying or selling government securities to financial institutions. Moving the federal funds rate up or down is the most common means the Federal Reserve utilizes to control monetary policy.

GOVERNMENT BORROWING BY COMPETITIVE BID:

<u>3 Month Treasury Bill</u>: These are sold by competitive bid at the New York Federal Reserve Bank; their purpose is to provide money to support the national debt. They are a barometer for the rise or fall of short term interest rates.

<u>30 Year Treasury Bond</u>: These are sold by competitive bid, and are a barometer for long term interest rates.

LOANS MADE BY COMMERCIAL BANKS:

<u>Prime Rate</u>: This is the interest rate that banks charge their larger commercial customers for short term loans. In a competitive marketplace, all banks tend to gravitate to the same prime rate. It gets a lot of attention because it is the benchmark used to set rates for many types of bank loans, such as mortgages and personal loans.

<u>Mortgage Rate</u>: This is the interest rate banks charge for home loans. There will be different rates depending on the life of the loan and the up-front costs, such as down payments and points. The term point is a loan fee, and one point is equal to one percent of the loan. Bankers and Realtors use the term points, because it is easier for consumers to swallow something called "points" during a mortgage negotiation than another heavy fee.

<u>Personal Loan Rates</u>: These are the interest rates set by each bank for making their loans for autos, installment purchases, personal loans, student loans, and such.

MONETARY DEPOSITS MADE IN COMMERCIAL BANKS.

<u>Checking accounts</u>: Normally these pay zero interest.

<u>Savings accounts</u>: These are at the bottom of the trickle-up process and normally pay the minimum interest of anything except checking accounts (or the money you "loan" to your children).

<u>Money market accounts</u>: Most of these deposits are reinvested by banks and mutual funds in 3 month Treasury bills or other short term securities, and they normally pay an interest under the rate of the 3 month Treasury bills.

<u>Certificates of deposit</u>: These deposits are accepted by the bank for various time periods, and the rate of interest paid will vary with the length of the deposit.

THE INTERPLAY OF INTEREST RATES:

Some interest rates are what you <u>pay</u> as an investor or consumer, while other rates are what you will <u>earn</u> as an investor. This interplay of interest rates begins with a "trickle-down" process that is the result of rates set by the Federal Reserve as they administer the nation's monetary policy.

SUMMARY

Interest rates evolve as a result of competitive pressures in a dynamic economy. Interest rates and the stock market have a tendency to move in opposite directions. A major input is supplied by the Federal Reserve as it sets monetary policy and utilizes interest rates that alter the money supply; thereby heating up or cooling down the economy. The Federal Reserve sets the monetary policy with a watchful eye on inflation, which is the culprit or bogey in the equation.

SEVEN: LIQUIDITY

Liquidity is another factor that causes the stock market to rise or fall. Federal Reserve Chairman, Allan Greenspan, described liquidity as "the excess cash sloshing around in the economy looking for a good buy."

We can predict that when liquidity is low the stock market suffers because potential buyers are cash poor. When liquidity is high and investors' pockets are full of dollars, they tend to buy stock and the market moves upward. While this may be true, how is an investor to know at any given time if liquidity is high or low? Therein lays a problem: we do not know how to measure it. Unfortunately, there are few yardsticks that do an adequate job; so it is difficult to get a true picture.

Since accurate measurement of liquidity is not possible, I will circle the subject with some background discussion of money supply, real interest rates, mutual funds, pension funds, etc., before I come back to the central theme and suggest a recipe to take aim on liquidity -- but don't hold your breath; in the end we must rely on "gut" feel.

THE LIQUIDITY KITTY: There is a huge pool of money generated each month available for investment that comes from such sources as pension funds, 401(k) s, insurance companies, money market mutual funds, and huge global slush funds. For example, the Public Employees Pension Fund for the State of Nevada (that my brother used to manage) has several million dollars of incoming money each month that it must invest somewhere. The neighboring state of California's similar pension (CALPERS) fund has many times that amount. How much would the insurance company, Aetna, have available in incoming money each month? There are thousands of 401(k) funds with cash looking for a home. What about the huge pool of global cash available to flow into the U.S. stock market? Here are a couple of "gee whiz" numbers from the past. In the week before Christmas of 1996, mutual fund investors poured 3.6 billion into the stock market, and for the full year of 1996, they pumped more than $200 billion into U.S. equity funds. That was fifteen years ago, and today you could add several "000s" to the numbers.

These pools of cash available to flow into -- or out of -- the stock market are staggering. They are a major causative factor that fueled the rising stock market of the 2000s. At any given time, how much of this sort of a liquidity pool is out there "sloshing around in the economy looking for a buy?" Let's start looking at some methods formerly used by the Federal Reserve to determine this.

<u>MONEY SUPPLY</u> The nation's money supply is part of the story of liquidity, so let's start there. Prior to the 1950's, the Federal Reserve's monetary policy focused on interest rates, and the level of the money supply was not an issue. It was not until 1959 that the Federal Reserve even started to publish data concerning the money supply, but since then it has measured this weekly by using the following categories:

<u>M1</u>: Currency, demand deposits, and other checkable deposits.

<u>M2</u>: M1 money supply plus money market bank accounts, savings and time deposits, and money market funds (excludes IRA's).

<u>M3</u>: M2 money supply plus large time deposits over $100,000, Eurodollars held by US residents overseas, Institutional funds, and money market funds.

<u>L:</u> M 3 plus non-bank holding of U.S. savings bonds, short term treasury securities, and commercial; so L is really the total.

In the 1960's, the Federal Reserve began to use money supply growth targets as one of its tools of monetary policy. This emphasis arose from a "Monetarist" theory, which held that if money supply grows two percent faster than the economy (as measured by the Gross Domestic Product), the economy will remain stable, and inflation will increase at an acceptable rate of 2% per year. A faster rate of money supply growth will lead to high inflation, and a lower rate may cause deflation, leading to a recession. The Federal Reserve monitored M2 closely, and it was a key element in their monetary policy decisions for many years. For that reason, a wise investor kept an eye on M2 for clues in the future direction of Federal Reserve policy to predict if interest rates would rise or fall.

Alan Greenspan backed away from this approach. In testimony before Congress in mid-1993, he said that the M2 had turned into a faulty indicator of the actual supply of money available to fuel the economy, and hence the pace of business activity. He indicated that instead of watching M2, the Federal Reserve would pay more attention to the real interest rate. It was never clear how much emphasis the Federal Reserve ever gave real interest rates, because there was seldom any additional comment on the subject.

REAL INTEREST RATE: Let's look at this concept. It is defined as the nominal interest rate minus the inflation rate (or interest rate minus inflation = real interest rate). If you receive 5% interest yield from an investment and the inflation rate is 5%, then it is breakeven, and you have earned nothing in terms of purchasing power; so the real interest rate is zero. The same is true for our nation's economy when the nominal rate of interest and inflation are the same.

In recent years, with both low interest rates and low inflation, the subject of real interest rate has fallen off the radar screen; but it is a fundamental logical relationship; so in future times it may still be lurking out there over the horizon as interest rates and/or inflation again begin to increase.

In his book, *The Age of Turbulence*, [4] Alan Greenspan made this observation: "When money supply grows at a faster rate than nominal GDP, that is tinder for inflation … In simple terms, the more money outstanding to purchase the flow of produced goods and services, the higher the average price."

When the Federal Reserve shifted from monitoring money supply to real interest rates, this did not indicate that money supply had become less important in the control of the economy: rather it was the realization that they had no accurate means to measure it. So instead of looking at some inaccurate causative factor, it watches for symptoms of high or low liquidity and the real interest rate is one such indicator.

MUTUAL FUNDS: Why had M2 become meaningless as a measure of liquidity? According to Greenspan, the biggest factor was the rise of mutual funds. Mutual funds were a major new development that began in the 1970s and 1980s. During the early1990's as interest rates fell, there was a change in where people placed their discretionary and investment cash. No longer was it at the bank. They pulled it out of bank deposits and CD's and moved it into mutual funds.

These mutual funds grew twelve-fold from 1980 to mid-1993. By the end of 1993, mutual funds had nearly two trillion in assets, approaching the national debt in size, and had become a major source of funds in the capital markets. In 1993 they were 33% of the overall stock market. At that time, if Congress had passed a law converting all mutual funds to the government, it could have pay off the national debt. That might have been a tough sell.

How does this relate to liquidity? Adding mutual funds to the mix increases the complexity of determining money supply growth and liquidity. Mutual funds are quite fluid because of the ease with which they can be converted to cash. Only a phone call by an investor is needed to transfer an entire portfolio into a money market fund or into cash by the end of the trading day, and a fund manager can perform virtually the same feat for an entire mutual fund. The result is that mutual funds have expanded the potential money supply and increased its fluidity. It has added immensely to the volatility of the market.

GLOBAL FUNDS: Another factor that affects liquidity is global funds, which will be mentioned here only briefly and discussed in more detail later. The day when financial markets ended at a country's border is long past. We now deal with a global market and must consider the potential money supply that flows across our borders, coming in to increase liquidity, or leaving our domestic market and creating potential havoc in the aftermath. In a global market, the challenge for the investor grows more complex.

SUMMARY:

The message to take from this section on liquidity is that even though there are few numbers for measurement, liquidity is an important causative factor in moving the stock market up or down. A successful investor must develop an intuitive, "gut" feel for liquidity.

EIGHT:
DOLLAR EXCHANGE RATE

During the 2008 meltdown, perhaps no economic factor had a bigger impact on the domestic stock market than the exchange rate in the global financial picture. It is a difficult subject to get one's arms around as exemplified by the controversy surrounding it. I will discuss generalities before I address the details of this complex subject, and I will start with a historical review.

In our global economy, stock markets have a world-wide clientele. Professor Martin Feldstein, Chairman of the Council of Economic Advisors in the Reagan administration, gave the following appraisal. [5]

"Until the decade of the 1980's it was common for Americans to ignore the international role of our economy. Imports and exports accounted for less than 10 percent of our gross national product, trade was approximately in balance, and international capital flows financed a very small portion of the net investment in the United States. ... The events of the 1980's changed all of that. The dollar rose more than 75 percent between 1980 and 1985, leading to a massive trade deficit and a correspondingly large capital inflow. By 1986, the trade deficit of the U.S. exceeded $170 billion or 4 percent of GNP, and was inflicting substantial pain on firms that exported to the rest of the world or that competed with imports from abroad. ... It was no longer possible to ignore the international environment within which the U.S. economy operated."

Now two decades later, the wise investor must manage his assets with one eye on the United States economy and the other looking at what is happening in the international arena. An important variable in the global economy is the dollar exchange rate. The investor can use it as a comparative guidepost; however, the value of the dollar is constantly changing because of international trade, and it will be different next month from what it is today.

Currency exchange transactions were handled by a fixed rate system for thirty years after World War Two. This was agreed to in 1944 at a meeting in Brenton Woods, a resort in New Hampshire, by the finance ministers and central bankers of all the Allied nations. It was agreed that exchange rates between nations would be based on a dual system of payments based on either gold or the U.S. dollar. If a country ran a trade deficit with another, it could settle this with a payment using either gold transfers or U.S. dollars. If a country ran out of gold reserves or dollars, it had to devalue its currency. The British, Germans, and French all had to do this at some time during the 1960s or 1970s.

As time went on during the post war era, the economy of the United States gradually lost its dominance. As a result of trade deficits, the gold reserves and currencies held by the United States gradually became depleted. Finally, two events took place that made the Brenton Woods agreement null and void. The first occurred in mid-1970 when President Nixon said the United States would no longer guarantee a transfer of gold in payment of debts. A second action by the United States was to abort the fixed rate of $35/ounce for gold. Until this time, it was unlawful for U.S. citizens to have gold except for teeth and jewelry. The government announced in 1977 that citizens could now purchase gold, and its price was free to float. Overnight, it jumped to $60/ounce and later to levels of $400/ounce. The effect of these two unilateral actions by the United States was to negate the Brenton Woods gold standard agreement, and it left the world's currencies to float and seek their own levels. At the outset for a number of years, they all floated against the value of the U.S. dollar, and that remains essentially true still today.

How much is a dollar worth in value against other currencies? That is an issue that determines to some degree the standard of living of people in the United States compared with other countries. When the dollar is strong, we can purchase more of those good things of life; however, a strong dollar makes our exports more expensive overseas, and our economy and employment levels suffer.

During the 1980s, cheap imports from abroad helped us maintain a higher standard of living than we could support on the basis of our own economy, but unemployment climbed higher at that time because we were unable to export our expensive products abroad. Protectionist pressures were building up in Congress.

Against this back drop in 1985, U.S. Secretary of Treasury, Jim Baker, organized a meeting in the Plaza hotel in New York City of the Central Bankers and Finance Ministers from five countries: France, Germany, Japan, the United Kingdom, and the United States. These countries agreed in what is now called the "Plaza Accord", to drive down the value of the U.S dollar. This action was, in effect, a programmed devaluation of the U.S. dollar. The United States went along with this agreement as a way to improve our export business and get a better balance of payments. The action headed off protectionist legislation that was under consideration by the Democratic controlled Congress. In less than three years, the G7 (later expanded from 5 to 7 and now up to 20 nations) pushed the dollar down 50% against major currencies. Here are some historical values in $ U.S of the German deutsch mark, Japanese yen, British pound, Chinese yuan, and European euro.

	DM	YEN	POUND	EURO	YUAN
1970	3.64	358			
1975	2.62	306			
1980	1.97	210			
1985	2.51	202			
1990	1.50	143	0.61	0.84	4.73
1995	4.20	361	0.64	0.82	8.46
2000	2.13	107	0.61	0.98	8.28
2005	EURO	102	0.53	0.74	8.28
2010		93	0.62	0.69	6.83

What were some of the effects of this devaluation of the dollar? When the dollar can buy only 143 yen in 1990, as compared to the 306 yen in 1975, it means that the Japanese are able to trade yen for dollars and come to America and buy property that now costs them less than half as much. That is what they did in the late 1980's, including the purchase of such items as the Empire State Building and the Pebble Beach Golf Club.

More significantly, it meant that they could purchase more stock in

American corporations and become major players in our stock market. They also invested heavily in our treasury bills that pay 7% interest at a time when their yen could only get a 3% yield. The Japanese investor became a major purchaser of our U.S. debt instruments that were a principle means the United States used to finance the national debt. Then the Japanese financial system collapsed because of other reasons, and the yen virtually disappeared from our radar screen.

The currency of the European Common Market is the euro that was officially adopted in 1995. Since that time it has made a remarkable impact on the global picture as the second largest reserve currency and the second most traded currency in the world after the U.S. dollar. As of June 2010, with more than €800 billion in circulation, the euro is the currency with the highest combined value of banknotes and coins in circulation in the world, having surpassed the U.S. Dollar. In recent years, the Chinese yuan has gradually become one of the more important currencies because of the booming economy in China, and the considerable amount of the U.S. Foreign Debt it is now financing.

When the U.S. dollar becomes stronger against the euro and other foreign currencies will that be good or bad for our economy? Here are some possible impacts:

If you want to travel in Europe or overseas, that will be a good time because your dollar goes further.

If you are a businessman and trying to export your product overseas, it will be tougher, because foreigners will have to pay more in real terms for your products.

If you are importing products from overseas, it is good because you can get more products for the same money.

If you are unemployed and looking for a job, a strong dollar will be a hindrance because American factories will be under-utilized and need fewer workers.

SUMMARY:

The U.S. $ exchange rate is an important factor for investors, but its impact is not always immediately apparent. The effect of changes may be experienced first in our domestic business cycle because of the impact on exports or imports, which will either heat up or cool down. There are no consistent guidelines suggesting whether to "buy" or "sell", but the investor must be aware of what is going on in the global economy, because it may well lead to a rise or fall in the U.S. stock market.

NINE:
GROWTH DOMESTIC PRODUCT

In previous chapters we discussed the primary movers of the economy, which are:

> Corporate earnings
> Inflation
> Interest rates
> Liquidity
> Exchange rate

These are impacted by other things that influence or cause changes; these secondary elements include such things as the following:

> Gross Domestic Product (GDP)
> Psychology of market participants.
> Price/Earnings ratio
> Consumer Confidence Level
> Business Cycle
> Unemployment
> Monetary policies
> Fiscal policies
> National Debt
> Mutual Funds
> Derivatives, Credit Swaps, hedge funds, etc.

The most important of these is the Gross Domestic Product (GDP). It is a benchmark that measures the health of the economy and is computed once each quarter by the U.S. Department of Commerce. It is an attempt to corral all the goods and services produced domestically and measure the rate of growth or decline. Because of the difficulty in collecting all the data on a timely basis, the initial report is often in error; so revised figures come out over the next several months or quarters.

History tells us that the economies of industrialized countries can achieve an annual growth rate of about three percent when all the resources are fully employed. This is over a long-term period when the year-to-year recessions and recoveries have been averaged out. Some third world emerging economies that started from a lower base have been able to sustain much higher growth rates.

These are three basic causes of economic growth, which are:

A rise in the productivity due to such things as better utilization of capital equipment.

An increase in available resources such as more workers moving into the work force, or new natural resources are developed or discovered like a new oil field.

Technological change created by inventions or developments that create new efficiencies in resources.

There are other things that hinder growth, such as:

Inflation, which undermines enterprise.

Unemployment, which under-utilizes the work force.

A restrictive monetary policy.

Obsolescence of resources and the tools of production.

Restrictive environmental controls.

Chart #4 shows the Gross Domestic Product (GDP) through the economic ups and downs of thirty years until 2008, which is plotted against the earnings/share of corporations.

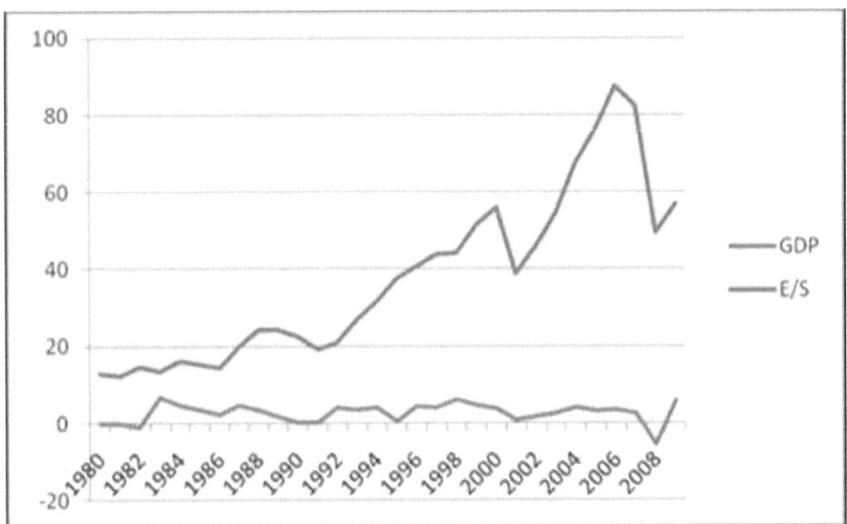

CHART 4: S&P INDEX AND GROSS DOMESTIC PRODUCT

In 2010 the GDP of the U.S. economy was roughly $12,200 trillion. The weak correlation between GDP and corporate earnings is a surprise. This is a bit difficult to explain since logic would suggest that when the economy is rising or falling, corporate earnings will also rise or fall in lock step. To some extent this is true with a lag in time, and a strong economy does create the environment in which corporations can improve their earnings; however, well managed companies can react with adjustments to their work force, factory utilization, inventories, and other factors to keep a healthy bottom line through good times and bad.

How the investor should utilize the GDP results is questionable. An improving economy usually means improving corporate earnings, which means higher stock prices. This may be true in the long term; however, history tells us that the correlation between the stock market and the economy is not close. We would not have had the long bull market during the 1980s without the underlying GDP growth rate early in the decade that averaged above 3 %; however, as the GDP growth rate petered out and went into recession, the stock market continued to rise to historic highs. So while the economy must be healthy to prop up the market, its short term effect is not always predictable.

Why is this so? One reason is that good management can often generate respectable corporate earnings even during hard times. Another reason is that investors' use their crystal ball and discount the effects of swings in the GDP well ahead of events – normally by at least 6 months. Also, the P/E

31

Ratio may grow higher as a result of investor speculation about predicted good time ahead.

SUMMARY:

Economic growth as measured by the GDP is a secondary market factor that should be monitored, but not reacted to unless it has a predictable impact on one or more of the primary market factors.

TEN:
THE BUSINESS CYCLE

Now we will look at the business cycles that occur in the economy, and their affect on the stock market. The term suggests a merry-go-round, but a better analogy to business activity is the traffic pattern well known to any commuter. I commuted on a busy freeway in Los Angeles for three years and left home at 6 AM traveling the freeway at 65 mph. Then along the way the flow of traffic gradually slowed, crawled bumper-to-bumper, sometimes stopped completely, and then gradually picked up speed again to 65 mph. My speed varied from standstill to 65, but averaged about 35 mph.

We can relate this traffic measured in miles per hour to economic activity measured by the Gross Domestic Product. The GDP in the United States has an average of 2% growth per year over many decades. This rate of economic growth is a phenomenon that is fueled by population growth with the resultant needs of people for products and services, plus the greater utilization of resources. The rate of growth is not steady, but surges above and below the overall 2% trend in a series of peaks and valleys with recessions dropping into a valley and expansions climbing up the hill.

Is all of this just theory, or do business cycles actually exist in the U. S. economy? The following Chart #5 provides a positive answer. It is a graphic picture of Gross Domestic Product over a 36 year time span as it cycles through the peaks and valleys of a number of business cycles.

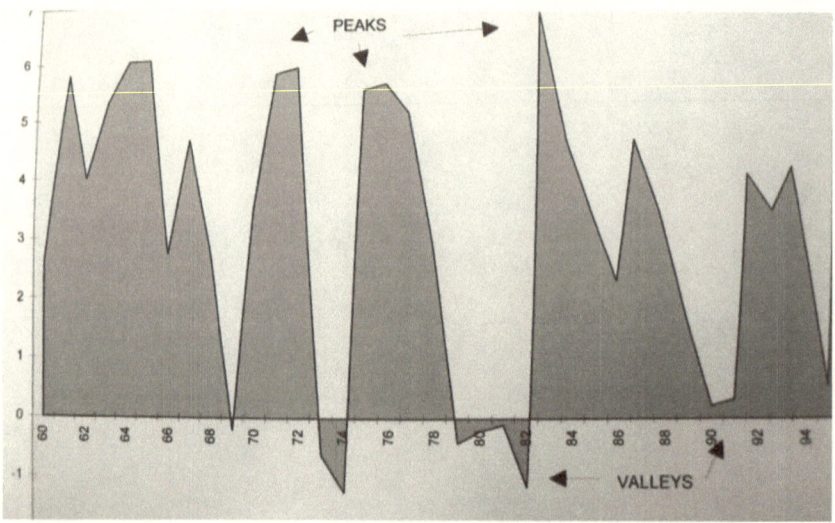

CHART # 5   BUSINESS CYCLES and GDP

Some of the characteristics of recessions and expansions are well understood; let's look at what is known.

THE BUSINESS EXPANSION: The expansion phase of the business cycle occurs after the traffic jam has been passed, and the auto begins to pick up speed. The expansion phase is the norm and this surge in economic growth is often fueled by the following:

1. An improvement in the productivity: workers become more productive and equipment becomes better utilized.
2. An increase in available resources: workers move into the work force with population growth, new resources such as an oil field are discovered, or management increases their capital spending with the expectation of better times ahead.
3. Technological change: developments such as those in computer technology that create rapid improvements in efficiency at the work station.

There is a synergy among these economic factors, and each provides positive reinforcement to the others. As more people become employed there is more buying power, and this leads to the need for more goods and services in a snowballing of growth factors. The result is an increase in business activity at a greater pace than the overall 2% GDP trend line.

As this expansion phase proceeds, there are some things happening with unemployment and inflation that gradually develop into negatives.

These will ultimately bring the expansion to an end and set the stage for a downturn in the economy. Unemployment rates are reduced during the expansion as the economy heats up and more jobs are created. An economist named Okun identified a historical pattern for this, now called Okun's law, which showed that for every 2 ½ % of GDP above the growth trend line there is a one percent decline in unemployment.

Unfortunately, the Phillips curve, which we will look at in the chapter on unemployment, comes into play. The improvement in employment will lead to increased inflation. The steps taken to counteract the growth of inflation will bring the business expansion to a standstill.

THE BUSINESS RECESSION: Now, let's look at the recessional phase. We reach the point on the freeway where the traffic jam begins. Economic growth slows to a crawl. Inflation with its resultant increase in interest rates is the bogie that normally causes most business recessions, but this is sometimes interwoven with other complexities. There are three categories of causes of recessions:

1. Internal causes such as changes in money supply, investment needs, wage rate demands, or lack of spending due to loss of consumer confidence.
2. External causes such as war, OPEC oil embargoes, and restrictive import-export policies.
3. Political activities such as tax increases, monetary or fiscal policy changes, or other activities that may have been manipulated as a result of politics.

Just as it is difficult in the commuting process to detect that a traffic jam is ahead on the freeway that is also true for recessions. Some triggering event, sometimes rather obscure, causes a pause in some aspect of business activity and a snowballing begins as negatives are accentuated. Here are some causes of recessions:

The recession in 1969 was caused by what is now called a "credit crunch". A tight-fisted monetary policy by the Federal Reserve created a lack of money supply, brought capital investment to a halt, and created a loss of consumer confidence, which reduced consumption. It developed slowly and the cause was so obscure that the recession came and was cured by the Federal Reserve with little fanfare.

The 1973 recession began with a bang when OPEC started the oil embargo that shot fuel prices upward and created an immediate increase in inflation.

The recession of 1989 was also obscure and remains controversial. The underlying cause was excessive spending and rising debt in government, corporate, and private sectors that built up during the Reagan years that created excessive inflation.

The recession of 2008 came with the financial meltdown of the nation's economy. It was caused by a combination of over-leverage, excessive risk-taking by financial institutions, a housing bubble, and the lack of sufficient reserves by the banking sector. The triggering event was an increase in unemployment when people lost their jobs and were unable to maintain the mortgages they had undertaken with insufficient collateral. Then the mortgage defaults and foreclosures began.

Business cycles are like last Sunday's football game; the best quarterbacking can be done on Monday morning. A recession is declared to officially exist when the GDP has a negative growth for two consecutive quarters. Some recessions are successfully reversed before growth has dropped to the level where an "official" recession is said to exist. The following table is a list of business cycles and shows some statistics for the recessions and recovery phases of each. During the recession, economic growth slows and inflation is high. Then the Federal Reserve delivers the inflation-control medicine to provide a cure.

HISTORY OF RECENT BUSINESS CYCLES

RECESSION PHASE				RECOVERY PHASE		
	GDP	INFLATION			GDP	INFLATION
			1960-64		6%	1%
1965-68	0%	6%	1969-72		6%	3%
1972-73	1%	12%	1974-76		6%	5%
1977-79	1%	13%	1982-87		7%	4%
1989-91	1%	6%	1992		4%	3 %
2008	5.4%	1%	2009		5.9%	2.7%

ECONOMIC POLICIES

The results of inflation and unemployment in the business cycle are a serious problem for nearly all governments; so various economic policies have been used in an attempt to maintain a stable economy and reduce the impact of business cycles. These approaches include the Monetarist, Keynesian, Free Market, and Supply Side. Let's look at these economic policies.

MONETARISM: This was an economic theory advanced during the 1950's by Milton Friedman and other economists. Their emphasis was on money supply. They argued that if the money supply grew at a two percent faster rate than the economy, the economy would remain relatively stable and inflation would increase at an acceptable rate of 2% per year. A faster rate of money supply growth would lead to high inflation and a lower rate to deflation, which would lead to a recession.

In the monetarist approach, the control is through the use of raising or lowering interest rates to alter the money supply. Paul Volcker, the Federal Reserve Chairman from 1979 to 1987, was a monetarist who used these policies to solve the high inflation of the late 1970's and early 1980's. Interest rates actually climbed to 19% before the money supply targets were accomplished and inflation was brought under control. In the public perception, Volcker went from a piranha at the outset of utilizing this strategy to a hero once it proved successful in conquering inflation.

KEYNESIAN: This was an economic theory advanced by Keynes, an Englishman, who was a dominant economist for the first half of the 20th century. His ideas gained much prominence during the Great Depression of the 1930s that gripped the United States and most western countries. His solution was for government to intervene in the natural business cycle to reduce unemployment by expanding the aggregate demand for products. The U. S. government attempted to prime the economic pump by massive public works programs such as the WPA and CCC, which put people back to work, raised aggregate demand, and attempted to move the business cycle from stagnation out of the depression. The success of this policy was not determined because World War two intervened in the process.

FREE MARKET: This is an economic theory that lets the market place have free rein and permits the underlying forces to achieve stability. The approach presupposes that counter-balancing forces will come into play and create stability when the market veers too far in either the expansive or contracting direction. The Federal Reserve that had followed a Keynesian approach to monetary control for several decades adopted a free market policy at the time of the presidency of Gerald Ford, who opposed regulation of financial markets. The end result of these unregulated free market policies was a major cause of the 2007 meltdown of our financial system. The triggering event was an increase in unemployment that caused an epidemic of mortgages falling into default, and then the financial system fell into recession when the housing bubble burst.

Alan Greenspan, who was the Federal Reserve chairman for many years prior to 2006, was a proponent of the Free Market theory; but in hindsight after the financial meltdown, he testified to congress that he now felt the theory was flawed and there was need for some degree of regulation of financial markets.

SUPPLY SIDE ECONOMICS: This is the economic policy used by President Reagan, which was called "voodoo" economics by political adversaries at the time. It received much media hype in 1981 as his administration got started. Supply side economists place heavy stress on the effect of taxation in determining the behavior of the economy. The proponents argue that tax cuts will promote growth by affecting savings and investments. The theory is that the benefits the wealthy and corporations receive with tax cuts trickle down to the masses and create growth throughout the economy. It has been nicknamed "trickle down" economics.

The supply side economic fiscal policy of the Reagan administration occurred at the same time as a massive government spending program for a defense buildup. Growth was stimulated with an increase in spending and reduced taxes, but the deficit climbed to excessive levels during the Reagan administration. During the following administration of President Bush, the supply side economic approach was abandoned when the huge federal deficit came into focus, then a tax increase was passed into law and this action marked the official demise of supply side economics.

BUSINESS CYCLES AND THE STOCK MARKET

Does the stock market have a cyclical pattern that matches the business cycle? Surprise! The answer is no. We find that stock market upturns occur only when GDP is healthy; however, the correlation between the stock market peak's and valleys with business cycles is not close. There are several reasons for this such as time lags that exist between cause and effect, corporate earnings developed by good management even during recessional periods, and investors' use of crystal balls to discount market events well in advance.

THE INSTANT BEAR MARKET Two terms frequently used by investors are a market "correction", which is a substantial drop that is a one-day event; and a "bear" market, which is a gradual slide over a longer time of months or years. A new "instant bear" phenomenon seems to have developed in which the entire bear activity is compressed to a few days and drops the market to a new level consistent with the economic reality in the business cycle. This may be the result of the following:

1. Computerized investing that uses preprogrammed logic that leads to quicker and more decisive action. For example, computer trading was tracked recently in which four cyclic tactical skirmishes occurred in the period of a single day.

2. Derivatives, hedge funds, the use of futures trading options, etc. There is now greater utilization of these investment devices that underlay the traditional stock market, and this provides a new type of quicker feedback on basic economic value. When the stock market prices are out of synch with the developing economy, the challenge created in the futures market is likely to lead to a quick reaction.

3. The average investor has become more sophisticated as portfolios become managed by the professionals who are more likely to have investment strategies for swift and decisive action when values get out of line with economic reality.

There have been two recent examples of these instant bear markets during the long bull market that started in 1982. The first was the crash of October 1987 when the market lost 30 % of its value almost overnight and brought P/E ratios from over 20 to l2. The second occurred in March 1994 when the market lost 8 % of its value in a few days and P/E ratios fell from 23 to l8. In each instance, the market was brought back to economic reality almost overnight rather than through the gradual bear market slide process.

The instant bear market represents a new peril. Investors must recognize when the market is out of synch with the economy, have a game plan ready for action, and beat the bear to the punch; otherwise, they may see a substantial part of their portfolio evaporate almost overnight.

SUMMARY

1. The business cycle is a natural economic phenomenon in

which the rate of business activity surges above and below a trend line of 2% annual growth.

2. Inflation is a major bogie that creates havoc and adds to instability in the business cycle.

3. Various monetary policies have been used in an attempt to maintain economic stability: Monetarism, Free Market, Keynesian, and Supply Side.

4. The smart investor keeps an eye on the business cycle and attempts to position investments accordingly. This is easier said than done.

ELEVEN:
PSYCHOLOGY IN THE ECONOMY

While the five primary parameters in the economy can be measured with benchmarks, an intangible parameter is the psychology of consumers and investors. It is their perception of the economy and how they may react. While some of these things are difficult to quantify, two that can be measured are the Consumer Confidence Level and the Price/Earnings Ratio.

The stock market sometimes displays activity that defies logic; it will suddenly rise or fall for no apparent reason, and we scratch our heads to understand why. The next day we read in the newspaper it is attributed it to something we find hard to believe. Many economic decisions spring from the gut, and nowhere is it written that they must always be rooted in logic? Some patterns come from the psychology of the investor, and we need to understand these to be successful in the market.

CONSUMER CONFIDENCE INDEX [6]

The U.S. Consumer Confidence Index is designed to measure consumers' confidence for their optimism on the state of the economy. It is measured monthly by The Conference Board, an independent research organization that conducts a survey based on 5,000 households. It is based on consumers' opinions on current conditions and future expectations. An increased consumer confidence suggests economic growth ahead and consumers will be spending money with higher consumption. Decreasing consumer confidence implies slowing economic growth in which consumers are likely to decrease their spending.

Each month the Conference Board asks five questions of the respondents' about the following:

> Current business conditions
> Business conditions for the next six months
> Current employment conditions.
> Employment conditions for the next six months.
> Total family income for the next six months.

Survey respondents are asked to answer each question as "positive", "negative", or "neutral". These are then compared against a baseline that was established in 1985. Manufacturers, retailers, banks, and the government monitor changes in the Index to include it in their decision-making processes.

This Consumer Confidence Index that is a psychological survey of a cross-section of the nation's households is widely accepted as a valid response, and it often leads to proactive measures in the investment community. A similar and well-established index that also measures consumer confidence is the University of Michigan Consumer Sentiment Index.

THE S&P 500 PRICE/EARNINGS RATIO

The Price/Earnings Ratio (P/E) is another measurement tool that is often utilized by investors to gauge the psychology of the investment community. The (P/E) is the ratio between the price of a stock and its earnings. Many investors look at this number for an individual company to decide if its earnings adequately reflect support for the price of a share of that company's stock. Other investors look at the number for the broader S&P 500 Index to gage the earnings for the overall market. The earnings is normally based on the earnings of the <u>past</u> year, but sometimes other time periods are used, such as the projected earnings for the forecasted <u>next</u> year; so using the number calls for some investigation to determine which time period is used.

The average P/E for the S&P 500 Index over the past 50 years is 15.5. This means that on average, the price paid for a share of stock in an S&P 500 Index fund is 15.5 times its earning over the past year.

The Price/Earnings Ratio is utilized by many investors as the degree of confidence by the investing community in an individual company or in the S&P 500 Index.

The P/E is a rough measure of the cost of the stock relative to the years for a payback. It can be interpreted as the "number of years of earnings to pay back the purchase price". [7] While this interpretation is only marginally accurate, a P/E of 18 would suggest that 18 years of earnings at the same level would be needed to pay for a share of the stock.

Some guidelines commonly used to help interpret the value of the Price/Earnings Ratio are the following:

0-10 Either the index is undervalued or the earnings are thought to be in decline.

10-17 A Price/Earnings ratio in this range may be considered fair value.

17-25 Either the Index is overvalued or earnings have increased since the last figures were published.

25+ The Index may have high future growth in earnings or subject to a "speculative bubble".

These patterns of investor behavior are based on actual history, and we should utilize them in understanding the stock market.

SUMMARY:

The stock market sometimes displays activity that defies logic or we find difficult to understand. Psychology and investor confidence are important factors. The market may suddenly rise or fall for no apparent reason and we scratch our heads trying to understand why? Many economic and stock market decisions spring from the gut, and nowhere is it written that they must always be rooted in logic.

TWELVE:
UNEMPLOYMENT

Unemployment is personal and traumatic. There is a common saying: "When your neighbor loses his job that is a recession; when you lose your job that is a depression." The Great Depression of the 1930s was properly named, because my dad lost his job when the markets crashed and his Camp Crook Bank was closed; but the 2007 Financial Meltdown was only a recession, because all members of my family remained employed.

Sociologists have found the three most traumatic events in a person's life are the death of a spouse, divorce, and loss of a job.

Unemployment is often an economic death sentence. People remain unemployed for various reasons:

- They are qualified for work but no jobs exist.
- Jobs are available but involve a lower rate of pay.
- Requires skill the person lacks.
- A spouse remains employed with less incentive for the other to seek work.
- Jobs may be available elsewhere but the worker is unwilling to move.

So unemployment has these and many other causes. An otherwise healthy economy does not always provide full employment. Companies watch their bottom line and labor is a major cost, so well-run companies will operate with the minimum labor force needed for their business. In early 2007, unemployment was at 5% and the nation's workforce was engaged in highly productive output; then the financial meltdown forced companies to cut their labor force, and unemployment quickly rose to

10%. The economy improved during the following years, but companies continued to operate with a lean workforce. A robust economy must create a consumer need before employment will return to the former levels of 5-6% -- if it ever does.

While unemployment takes a harsh toll on the individual and his family, it has less impact on the stock market. A high level of unemployment is often favorable to the stock market because it holds down the level of inflation.

While it would seem simple for a government to do the things that maintain full employment, history indicates that stabilizing both employment and the economy at the same time is difficult to accomplish. Why? <u>Inflation is the bogie that causes a problem in maintaining full employment</u>. The administration must often choose between two evils: high unemployment or high inflation. There is a natural seesaw or political cycle affecting the economy that is dominated by events in the workplace. This is the process:

1. With high unemployment during a poor economy, workers are willing to accept less pay to keep a job.
2. A new administration is elected on the promise to reduce unemployment. They enact programs to heat up the economy, create jobs, and then unemployment declines.
3. After the work force is back on the job, the unions are in a stronger bargaining position for higher wage demands. Since companies are making higher earnings, they raise pay scales to maintain a stable work force. When this occurs without a corresponding increase in worker productivity, the result is higher inflation.
4. The higher inflation causes the Federal Reserve to increase interest rates, the economy cools, and unemployment increases.

This relationship between unemployment and inflation has been documented with a long history. A New Zealand economist, W.S. Phillips, looked at this in 1958 for the preceding century in the United Kingdom, and developed the following conclusion: "The higher the rate of unemployment, the lower the rate of increases in money wages, or in other words, there is a tradeoff between wage inflation and unemployment."

This relationship is what has come to be called the Phillips Curve. It indicates when the rate of unemployment increases, inflation is decreased, and visa versa. Within the United State's *economist academe*, there is debate over the validity of the Phillips Curve's relationship. The next chart #6 addresses this question with a 30 year comparison of unemployment and inflation in the United State's economy. If the Phillips Curve is valid, then we should expect to see that the two curves are opposites of each other; when one goes down, the other rises. As you will see, there does seem to be some inverse relationship between unemployment and inflation; so the Phillips curve is valid for the U.S. economy. The relationship is less prominent at times when inflation was held captive to the cost of OPEC oil, rather than to wage rate increases. In more recent years the relationship is also less clear because of the weakness of the labor movement in the United States. However, even with these factors, a pattern becomes evident that the Phillips Curve is somewhat valid during the past 30 years in the United States economy.

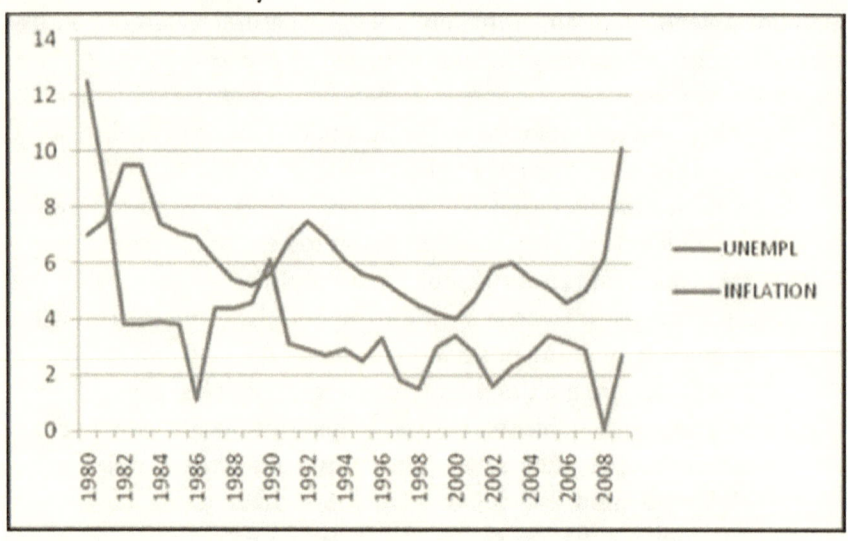

CHART #6:   INFLATION AND UNEMPLOYMENT

SUMMARY:

History supports the unfortunate fact that employment sometimes has an inverse relationship with the economy because of inflation. When the economy heats up and the level of employment improves, an increase in inflation is often the result and may be waiting just over the horizon.

The good social feeling that comes from a lower rate of unemployment is often a warning to the investor of higher inflation, higher interest rates, and a falling stock market ahead.

THIRTEEN:
U. S. FISCAL POLICY

Fiscal policy is the use of government expenditures and revenue collection to influence the economy. [8] It is controlled in the United States government by the congress that passes legislation involving taxation and expenditures; and the executive branch that signs these into law, executes, and administers the law. Governments use fiscal policy to influence the level of aggregate demand in an effort to achieve its economic objectives of price stability, full employment, and economic growth.

For much of our nation's history, the annual budget, spending levels, and size of the National Debt were ho-hum topics that seldom became a major political issue, but in recent decades they have become front page news. In times past it was generally understood that spending should be kept within the limits that revenue would support; however, that perception has gradually eroded both in citizens' private lives where living in debt has risen sharply, and at the government level where our nation spends substantially more than it raises in taxes.

THE BUDGET:

The annual budget is the initial step in the nation's fiscal process. Each year, the President submits the administration's proposed budget to Congress as required by the Budget and Accounting Act of 1921. To some extent, our modern budget is fiction because it does not contain some of the largest areas of spending, which includes the entitlement programs of Social Security, Medicare, and Medicaid. These are funded by permanent appropriations and are considered mandatory spending according to the

1997 Budget Enforcement Act. They are called "entitlements," because people meeting relevant eligibility requirements are legally entitled to benefits. With the strong support of the majority of Americans, these programs continue to exist, but due to rising spending and lack of tax revenue, they have created stress in the nation's fiscal affairs.

FEDERAL SPENDING

The following is the spending of the federal government for the year 2010:

Social Security	$695 Billion
Department of Defense	664
Other federal departments	662
Other mandatory programs	571
Medicare	453
Medicaid	290
Interest on National Debt	164
Other	53
TOTAL	$3,552 Billion

The category of "Other federal departments" is 19% and includes spending for all the twenty-five federal departments except for the Defense Department; so eighty percent of the nation's annual spending is for entitlements, defense, and things other than running the programs of the federal departments.

Going back in history to the 1930's when the Social Security program was first enacted into law, the growth of social programs has created political controversy that has generally followed party lines. The Democratic Party has pushed for new social programs such as Social Security and Medicare that increase the spending level, while the Republican Party has opposed raising taxes to pay for the programs; hence, this created an increase in the National Debt. Yet despite the traditional party lines, surprisingly, the greatest increases in the debt occurred during the fiscally conservative Republican administrations of Ronald Reagan and George H. Bush when it quadrupled, and then increased again during the administration of George W Bush as a result of defense spending for the wars in Iraq and Afghanistan that were not paid for with a raise in taxes.

In 2010, the spending level of the United States was 25% of Gross Domestic Product (GDP), roughly $3,550 billion. If the current tax revenue level remains the same, then spending must be reduced to 19% of

GDP to balance the budget, or to $2,698 billion, a reduction in spending of $852 billion. That will be tough to accomplish.

REVENUE (TAXES)

During 2010, the federal government collected $2.2 trillion in tax revenue. Primary receipt categories included individual income taxes (42%), Social Security taxes (40%), and corporate taxes (9%). Tax revenues have averaged approximately 18.3% of Gross Domestic Product (GDP) over the past 40 years. [9]

Regardless of the cost for running the Federal Department programs, the defense spending, entitlement and mandatory costs in the budget must all be raised by taxes, or the difference borrowed, raising the National debt.

Tax revenues are significantly affected by the economy. Recessions typically reduce government tax collections as economic activity slows. For example during 2009, the government collected about $400 billion less than the year before in 2008. Individual income taxes declined 20%, while corporate taxes declined 50%. At 15% of GDP, the 2009 collections were the lowest level of the past 50 years. [10] The revenue collected is also affected by demographic trends. The number of workers continues declining relative to those receiving benefits. For example, the number of workers per retiree was 5.1 in 1960; this declined to 3.3 in 2007 and is projected to decline to 2.1 by 2040. [11] That means fewer workers are contributing part of their income into the Social Security Trust Fund. This unfavorable combination of demographics and per-capita rate increases is expected to drive both Social Security and Medicare into large deficits during the 21st century. These programs may be fiscally unsustainable as presently structured due to the extent of future borrowing and related interest required to fund them

THE U.S. NATIONAL DEBT.

Chart # 7 shows the rise in the National Debt. It remained low prior to the 1980's until the Reagan and Bush administrations when costs rose sharply in support of a buildup of the military with no new tax revenue in support. It continued to climb sharply again starting in 2002 due to the Iraq and Afghanistan wars with no offsetting tax revenue.

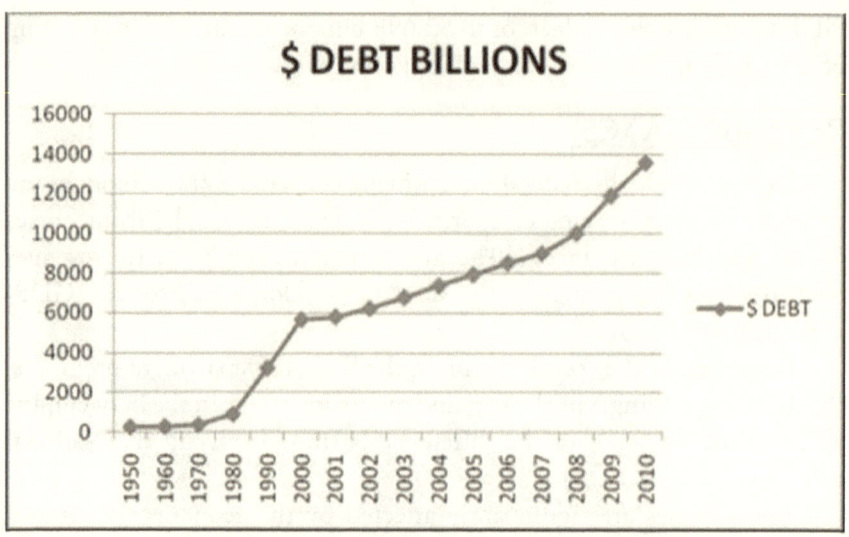

CHART # 7: NATIONAL DEBT IN $ BILLIONS

The National Debt is generally measured against the Gross Domestic Product (GNP) - - all the goods and services produced each year -- which compares the rise in debt to the state of the economy. A strong economy can support a heavier load of National Debt. Chart #8 below provides this comparison. The increase in debt during the 1940's is due to the huge costs of World War Two. The chart shows the increase of the 1980's during the administrations of Reagan and Bush, followed by a reduction during the Clinton years, and then the increase in debt during the George W Bush years beginning in 2005.

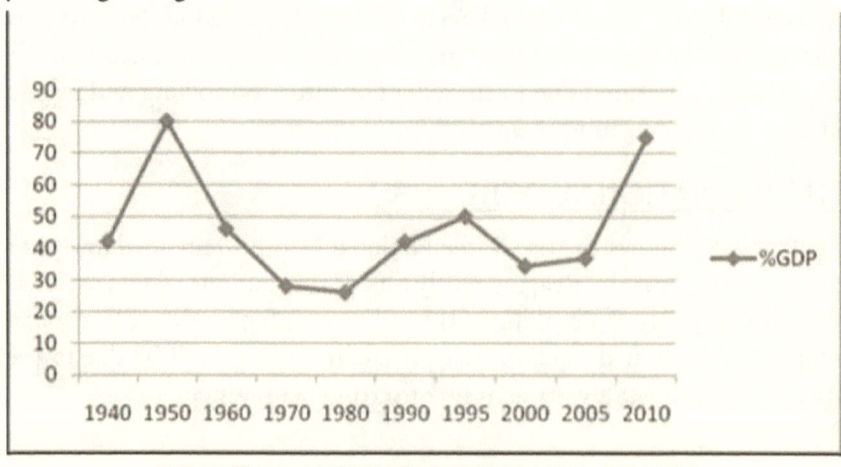

CHART # 8: NATIONAL DEPT AS % OF GDP

As of January 31, 2011, the "total public debt outstanding" was $14.13 trillion and was 96.4% of calendar year 2020's annual Gross Domestic Product (GDP) of $14.7 trillion. [12] This deficit has to be raised by the government by borrowing on the open market with bonds and Treasury bills at the prevailing rates of interest. We will pay these off when they become due by issuing more of the same to cover the principal, plus the interest due, and push the debt payback further down the road.

The Administration and Congress have several ways by which they can face this growing national debt. Here are the options:

1. Borrow from the future with the consequences of a larger debt as interest grows.
2. Let foreigners pay for it and accept the consequences of an eroded dollar in international trade.
3. Ignore it by printing money with the risk of increased inflation.
4. Reduce our spending level by cutting programs.
5. Increase revenue by raising taxes.

In actual fact, we have done a bit of all these things in recent years.

SUMMARY:

Let us now address the question of why the deficit will affect our investments: the reason is that how we address the problem will directly affect the primary parameters that drive the stock market, which are: inflation, interest rates, corporate earnings, liquidity, and $ Exchange rates

Each of these basic factors is affected in varying degrees, depending on whether, and how, we cut expenditures, raise taxes, or do nothing. The long term financial health of our nation and the value of your and my investments in corporate stock will hang in the balance.

FOURTEEN:
THE U. S. MONETARY POLICY

Monetary policy is the process by which the monetary authority of a country (its central bank) controls the supply of money. Monetary policy in the United States is controlled by the Federal Reserve System. It often targets a rate of interest for the purpose of promoting economic growth and stability. [13] Monetary policy is contrasted with fiscal policy, which refers to: taxation, government spending, and associated borrowing. The monetary policy is referred to as either being Expansionary or Contractionary. An Expansionary policy increases the total supply of money and is used to combat a recession by lowering interest rates to entice business into expanding. A Contractionary policy decreases the money supply and is intended to slow inflation in hopes of avoiding the deterioration of asset values.

The Federal Reserve is the central bank of our country. It was created in 1913 with the enactment of the Federal Reserve Act, largely in response to a series of financial panics, particularly a severe panic in 1907. Over time the roles and responsibilities of the Federal Reserve System has expanded and its structure has evolved. Events such as the Great Depression were major factors leading to changes in the system. Its duties today are to conduct the nation's monetary policy, supervise and regulate banking institutions, maintain the stability of the financial system and provide financial services to depository institutions, the U.S. government, and foreign official institutions.

The Federal Reserve System's structure is composed of a presidentially appointed Board of Governors, the Federal Open Market Committee

(FOMC), twelve regional Federal Reserve Banks, and numerous other private member banks. The FOMC is responsible for setting monetary policy and consists of all seven members of the Board of Governors and the twelve regional bank presidents. The Federal Reserve is independent within government in that its decisions do not have to be ratified by the President or anyone else in the executive or legislative branch of government. However, its authority is derived from the U.S. Congress and is subject to congressional oversight. Additionally, the members of the Board of Governors, including its chairman, are chosen by the President and confirmed by Congress. The original philosophy was that this maintained free banking by permitting the operation of a dual banking system within the American free enterprise economy. It was to exercise control over the nation's banking system, but had to accomplish this through a decentralized system in which membership by private commercial banks was voluntary.

We often hear reference to a "central" bank, and this refers to the twelve district Fed banks acting in unison under the direction of the Board of Governors. There have been many amendments that increased the scope of the Federal Reserve System, and it is now one of the most powerful forces in American and world-wide economics. Other countries also have central banks. The central bank in Germany, the Bundesbank, is a quasi-governmental institution similar to ours. The Bank of England is under the direct control of the British Parliament, and the Bank of Japan is under the direct control of the Japanese Government Ministry of Finance.

THE FEDERAL OPEN MARKET COMMITTEE

This is a powerful body within the Fed that meets once each six weeks, and sets the nation's monetary policy. This committee consists of the seven governors, plus five presidents from the twelve district banks. Daily operations are executed by a subcommittee of five.

After they determine what the overall monetary policy should be, they set targets and decide what sort of tactics will be used in open market transactions. The committee issues directives to the New York Federal Reserve Bank, which does the actual buying and selling of securities. It is these tactics that determine the interest rates. When the Fed enters the competitive market place with their checkbook open, what they want to accomplish will prevail. Who is going to bid against them?

The minutes of the meetings of the FOMC are kept as highly guarded secrets for some time after their meetings are held to avoid counter moves which would make the tactics less effective. It is sort of like calling the plays in the football huddle, then keeping them secret until they are executed as the play action develops..

Financial investors, stock brokers, and other paranoid Fed watchers keep an ear to the ground for any new murmur coming forth from this group, because they set the future course for interest rate changes and other actions that affect the economy. In more recent years they have relaxed this secrecy policy somewhat, since nothing in Washington is ever fully secret, and now issue vague hints at the close of the meeting such as: "Maybe", "We might", or "Who knows". Appendix C contains a typical report issued after a meeting of the FMOC,

ECONOMIC PHILOSOPHIES

The philosophies of the Fed have evolved over time. In recent decades the Fed has assumed a major role in maintaining a stable national economic growth. As a practical matter, the Fed cannot simultaneously set targets for both interest rates and money supply. Because they interact, it has to set targets for one and let the other seek the new level that will develop.

The philosophy for how this should be accomplished has varied with the different chairman. Some were "Keynesians", who rely heavily on interest rates to transmit the effect of monetary policy to the economy. Some were "monetarists", who believe that control of the nation's money supply is the essential element of control. Others take a pragmatic position to use whatever policy appears to be best in any given situation.

All U.S. Republican and Democratic administrations operated essentially with Keynesian economic philosophies from 1944 until 1975, when President Ford in a speech to a business audience promised, "I will take the shackles off American businessman and get the federal government out of your business, out of your lives, out of your pocketbook, and out of your hair as possibly I can." That was the point at which the United States government changed to a "Free Market" philosophy, which was adopted by all administrations from that time until the financial meltdown of 2007. Near the end of his administration, President Bush temporarily turned away from Free Market to a Keynesian economic policy with enactment of the $700 billion TARP program that he signed into law on October 3, 2008. He also had the support of Bernanke, Chairman of the Federal Reserve.

Each philosophy has its disciples. During the 1970's under Chairman Miller, a Keynesian, the Fed focused on interest rates. He was replaced in 1979 by Chairman Paul Volcker, who switched to a monetarist policy of targeting money supply. His philosophy was to tie central bank policy to money supply targets, and by a tightfisted control of the money, he moderated interest rates to suppress inflation.

Alan Greenspan was Fed Chairman from 1988 to 2006 and believed in a Free Market philosophy. When testifying before a congressional committee after he retired, Greenspan said in hindsight, "I always thought that in a Free-Market economy, it would be essentially self-policing, but I now see no alternative to the imposition of regulation over the institutions of our financial systems."

Bernanke became the chairman of the Federal Reserve System in 2006, and he presided over the financial meltdown that began the following year in 2007.

FEDERAL RESERVE TOOLS UTILIZED

The tools the Fed can use to stimulate or to retard the economy fall into the categories of reserve requirements, open market operations, discount rate changes, and federal funds rate changes. Here are their tools:

The Reserve requirement is the percentage of a commercial bank's deposits that they must keep in their vaults or on deposit at their district Fed bank. The more money they must leave inactive in their vault, the less they have available to loan, hence the less in circulation in the nation's money supply. This reserve requirement is the most powerful tool the central bank has; therefore changes are made rarely and with much discretion.

The Open Market operations involve the purchase and sale of government bills, bonds, and notes. These are administered through the New York Federal Reserve bank. By intervening directly in this commercial process as the "big kid on the street," the Fed has great impact in these markets.

The Discount Rate is the interest rate that member banks pay to borrow from the Fed. In a "trickle-down" process, the discount rate is at the top, because the Fed controls the money and this is where it starts. To increase the money supply and stimulate economic activity, the Fed will lower the rate, making borrowing more attractive for the commercial banks, and the Fed will reverse the process when it wants to cool the economy. The Federal Funds Rate has a similar effect as the discount rate, and is the most frequently used tool of the Fed in recent years. It is the rate banks charge one another for short term or over-night loans, and this can also be indirectly controlled by the Fed by buying or selling government securities to financial institutions.

THE FED INTERNATIONAL ROLE

The international role of the Fed is a new dimension. In recent years there has been an increasing need to control the value of the U. S. dollar in relation to foreign currencies in the best interests of our own domestic economic stability. The FOMC of the Fed undertakes transactions in foreign currencies in order to help safeguard the value of the dollar.

This international activity complicates the options available to the Federal Reserve. Such issues as international balance of payments and federal budget deficits become involved, and simplistic solutions that look only at domestic banking issues aren't realistic. With the world-wide economy becoming encumbered with political pressures at home and abroad, the task of maintaining stable growth becomes exceedingly complex.

SUMMARY

Monetary policy is the process by which the monetary authority of a country (its central bank) controls the supply of money. Monetary policy in the United States is controlled by the Federal Reserve. System. It often targets a rate of interest for the purpose of promoting economic growth and stability

The Federal Reserve System's structure is composed of a presidentially appointed Board of Governors, the Federal Open Market Committee (FOMC), twelve regional Federal Reserve Banks, and numerous other private member banks. The FOMC is responsible for setting monetary policy and consists of all seven members of the Board of Governors and the twelve regional bank presidents.

The Federal Reserve System in recent years has gradually become one of the most important institutions affecting our domestic economy and, indeed, the global economy.

FIFTEEN:
WHERE AND HOW TO INVEST

When I was a younger person working in a demanding executive job, I used a stockbroker to invest in various companies, often on my initiative and other times on the broker's recommendation. My investment activities were burdened with several realities:

1. I was submerged in a busy work-a-day job and had little time to devote to my personal investments.

2. I did not feel I had the expertise to make investment decisions even though I had a master's degree with a background in economics

3. Investments and the stock market were a game in which I had little genuine interest at that time in my life.

As a consequence, I was happy to find an investment counselor that I could hand the job to and also to utilize my company's 401k. Those who are still working in challenging, time consuming jobs may find themselves in the same boat and feel the need for similar assistance.

Where to invest? There are many options and at some time I have employed all of the following:

> Stockbroker
> Investment counselor
> 401(k)
> IRA
> Annuities
> Certificates of Deposit (CD's)
> Bonds

> Real estate
> Bank savings accounts
> Mutual funds

STOCKBROKER: I will not discuss this in any detail because there are others you can consult with more expertise than I have. While I still occasionally utilize a broker, I have little current experience and things have changed considerably in recent years.

INVESTMENT COUNSELOR: Through the years, I have utilized an investment counselor and this is a good way for most people to get started. However, it is difficult to know how to pick the right one, and a bad choice can cause problems. I would suggest the following:

> Conduct an initial interview and pursue their investment approach, and how they will interface with you -- who make what decisions?
> Review their background and experience.
> How and how much they will charge for their services?

My first experience with an investment counselor was rather poor. I was naïve and chose one that charged me on the basis of up-front fees for each transaction; you can predict the result. Fortunately, I had placed only a small part of my portfolio with that counselor and quickly exited the relationship. A major criterion I can now definitely recommend is that their fee should be on the basis of an annual fixed percentage of the total dollars in your portfolio with no other transaction fees.

401(k) : For those working in an organization where a 401(k) is available, this is normally one of the best investment opportunities.

It is a type of saving account that takes its name from the subsection 401(k) of the Internal Revenue Code. Employers can help their employee save for retirement while reducing taxable income, and workers can deposit part of their earnings into a 401(k) account and not pay income tax until the money is withdrawn later in retirement. Interest earned on money in a 401(k) account is never taxed before funds are withdrawn. Employers may choose to, and often do, match contributions that workers make. The 402(k) account is typically administered by the employer, while in the usual "participant-directed" plan the employee may select from different kinds of investment options. Employees choose where their savings will be invested, usually between a selection of mutual funds that emphasize stocks, bonds, money market investments, or some mix of the above. The 401(k) plans of many companies also offer the option to purchase the company's stock. The employee can generally re-allocate money among these investment choices at any time. [14]

IRA's: An Individual Retirement Arrangement (IRA) is a form of retirement that provides tax advantages for retirement savings. They were first initiated in 1974 and have been modified several times since, in 1981, 1986, and 2001. The Federal Act of 2001 broadened the type of funds that could be rolled into and also relaxed some rules. The IRA is held at a custodial institution such as a bank, brokerage, or mutual fund, and may be invested in anything that the custodian allows. When the custodial institution is a brokerage, it can invest in corporate stock. Transactions in the IRA account that include interest, dividends, and capital gains are not subject to federal income tax until withdrawn from the account

If a taxpayer expects to be in a lower tax bracket in retirement than during the working years, an IRA defers the tax to their advantage and the taxpayer gets the tax benefit immediately. There are two age-related disadvantages with IRA's: a 10% early distribution penalty if the participant is under the age of 59 ½ and a forced distribution that begins by age 70 ½.

Sheltered IRA assets can be moved in two ways between financial institutions: the receiving and distributing institutions can transfer assets between them directly by check, and a "rollover" transfer can be made by an individual participant to move IRA money between institutions. The rollover transaction must be completed within a span of 60 days for the funds to retain their IRA status, and this can be done only once every 12 months with the same funds.

After I retired and had money in both a 401(k) and also a lump-sum pension asset with my company, I was able to rollover both of these into IRA accounts. A majority of my investment portfolio since then has been primarily in IRA accounts, which has been a huge advantage for me from a tax standpoint. Now past the age of 70 ½, I must make forced distributions each year, but I am able to do this and pay these deferred taxes at my present lower tax bracket.

ANNUITIES: An annuity is a contract between you and an insurance company under which you make a lump-sum payment or series of payments. In return, the insurer agrees to make periodic payments to you beginning immediately or at some future date. Annuities typically offer tax-deferred growth of earnings.

There are generally two types of annuities -- fixed and variable. In a fixed annuity, the insurance company guarantees that you will earn a minimum rate of interest during the time that your account is growing. In a variable annuity you can choose to invest your purchase payments from among a range of different investment options, typically mutual funds. The rate of return will vary depending on the investment options you have selected. [15] The majority of customers use annuities only to accumulate funds free of income and capital gains taxes and to later take lump-sum withdrawals without using the guaranteed-income-for-life feature. [16]

I have an annuity with the California AAA insurance company, and for several years it has been returning me a substantially higher rate of interest than CD's or money market funds.

MUTUAL FUNDS: Mutual funds are modern phenomena that have transformed the role of investing for most individuals. Investors can be active in the stock market without the need for a broker to buy or sell, and they can personally manage their own portfolio. A mutual fund company is registered with the Securities and Exchange Commission (SEC) and must distribute its net income annually to its investors. Mutual funds came into existence when Congress passed the Securities Act of 1933, but initial interest was nil. A key factor increasing growth was in 1975 when Congress allowed individuals to open Individual Retirement Accounts (IRA's) in mutual funds. Since then the growth has accelerated and in 2007 there were 8015 mutual funds with combined assets of $12 Trillion. For comparison, in 2010 the total national debt of the United States is $12 Trillion, roughly the same amount as that invested in domestic mutual funds. The world-wide value of all mutual funds totals more than $26 Trillion. Why have they become so popular with individual investor's? Here are some advantages they offer:

> Diversification.
> Ease of investing.
> Dollar cost averaging.
> Good management costs.
> Investment expertise.

The following chart #9 shows the phenomenal growth until 1989 when the value on all funds reached $2.5 Trillion. If we were to extent the chart forward to 2010, the line representing the value would be 14 inches high, well off the top of the page. Mutual funds have, indeed, become a major factor in the domestic and world's investment picture.

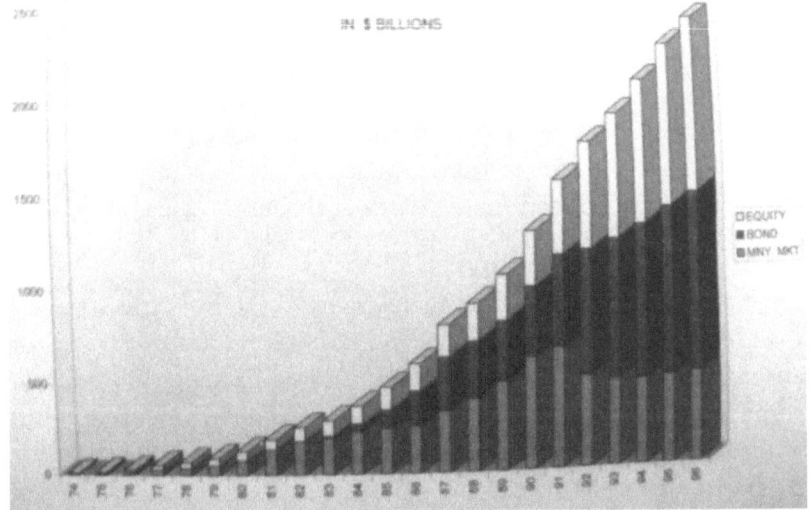

CHART #9: MUTUAL FUNDS GROWTH

Let's look at these benefits of mutual funds.

Diversification: It was Benjamin Franklin who said, "Don't put all your eggs in one basket." Mutual funds have a built-in diversification; the money in a single fund is spread through dozens of individual investments. The investor can include several different categories of funds such as a growth fund, money market fund, and global funds. I also invest in several mutual fund companies such as USAA and Vanguard, which is further diversification.

There are various rules concerning protection for fraud with investments in mutual funds or brokerage accounts, but in general it is wise to keep your total investment under $500,000 per account holder per account type. You may not become a victim like Bernie Madoff's clients, but there are plenty of other sharks in the ocean. The Securities Investor Protection Corp., or SIPC, is the organization that provides a safety net.

Ease of investment: Dealing with a mutual fund is user-friendly. After you send in the initial application, all subsequent matters can be handled by phone or over the internet.

Dollar Cost Averaging: Mutual funds are ideal for this means of investing. My method is to initially place money in a money market fund, and then transfer it to another fund when I feel the time for an equity investment is at hand.

Management Costs: These costs are less than for most other types of investments. The no-load funds do not incur costs other than an annual management fee. If it is an IRA account, there may also be a custodial fee. I previously invested in some funds that charged a front end "load" or brokerage fee, but I found from experience that these funds performed no better than my no-load funds. I now deal almost exclusively with no-load funds.

Investment Expertise: The fund manager picks the fund investments to buy and sell, determines the timing, and executes the strategy. Can a fund manager out-perform the market? Yes. If they take a high risk gamble and it turns out to be correct, they become a hero receiving media accolades. The conservative ones make less money in a rising market, but they are appreciated when the market falls. Some fund managers have a good batting average over a period of time.

Ease of Investing: A big advantage that mutual fund companies have carefully developed is that they are "user-friendly." This is important for an investor who is unfamiliar with all the investment jargon. It is easy to pick up the phone and talk to a representative who has been trained to be courteous and professional. Mutual funds have become a modern revolutionary development in the stock market and they are likely to remain a major player into the future years.

SUMMARY

Where to invest? There are many options and at some time I have employed all of the following: stockbroker, investment counselor, 401(k), IRA, annuities, certificates of deposit (CD's), bonds, real estate, bank savings accounts, and mutual funds.

With any investment there is always a trade-off between degree of risk and rate of return. An investor should consider their earning capacity and years to retirement and take into account their temperament. If they are a person who frets every time the stock market has a drop, then they should select conservative investments. On the other hand, if they have many working years ahead and their objective is to build a large nest egg and they are willing to endure the market's ups-and-downs, then they should look for investments that appear to have greater opportunity to achieve this.

SIXTEEN:
DERIVATIVES, HEDGING, ETC.

If you are like me, you have been exposed to a new vocabulary of financial terms in recent years; things we never previously heard about. What are derivatives? What is hedging -- or a hedge fund? Then there is the strangest of all: a debit default swap -- it sounds almost vulgar. While I have no personal experience with any of these things, I think I understand them after doing some research, and realize they may have been involved in some of my previous investments. I have also gained a new appreciation that these new tools are valuable innovations to our financial system. Let's start with derivatives, which could be described as the umbrella that contains many other types of investments under its shade.

A derivative is a financial agreement between two parties that has a value based on the expected future price movements of the asset to which it is linked -- called the underlying asset -- such as a share of stock or a currency. There are three major classes of derivatives: futures, options, and swaps. [17]

Futures are contracts to buy or sell an asset on or before a future date at a price specified today.

Options are contracts that give the owner the right, but not the obligation, to buy or sell an asset at a price specified at the time the parties enter into the agreement.

Swaps are contracts to exchange cash on or before a specified future date based on the underlying value of currencies, exchange rate, or other assets.

A derivative is not a stand-alone option since it has no value of its own. However, more common types have been traded on markets before their expiration date as if they were assets. Among the oldest of these are rice futures, which have been traded on the Dajima Rice Exchange since the early eighteenth century. [18]

Derivatives are used by investors to accomplish the following:

a. Provide leverage.

b. Speculate and make a profit if the value of the underlying asset moves the way they expect.

c. Hedge or mitigate risk in the underlying asset.

d. Obtain exposure to the underlying asset where it is not possible otherwise to trade in it.

e. Create option ability where the value is linked to a specific condition or event.

Derivatives allow risk related to the price of the underlying asset to be transferred from one party to another. For example, a wheat farmer and a miller could sign a futures contract to exchange a specified amount of cash for a specified amount of wheat in the future. Both parties have reduced a future risk: for the wheat farmer, the uncertainty of the price; and for the miller, the availability of wheat. However, there is still the risk that no wheat will be available because of events unspecified by the contract such as the weather, or that one party will renege on the contract. Although a third party, called a clearing house, insures a futures contract, not all derivatives are insured against counter-party risk.

Hedging also occurs when an individual buys an asset and sells it using a futures contract. The individual has access to the asset for a specified amount of time and can then sell it in the future at a specified price. Derivatives can serve other legitimate business purposes such as when a corporation borrows a large sum of money at a specific interest which resets every six months, so the corporation will then buy a forward rate agreement (FRA), which is a contract to pay a fixed rate of interest.

Derivatives can also be used to acquire risk, rather than to insure or hedge against risk by speculating on the value of the underlying asset; hence, betting that the party seeking insurance will be wrong about the future value of the underlying asset.

HEDGING:

In commerce, hedging is a method by which traders use two counterbalancing investment strategies so as to minimize any losses caused by price fluctuations. It is most commonly used by traders in the commodities market. Typically, it involves a trader contracting to buy or sell one particular thing at the time of the contract and also to buy or sell the same commodity at a later date.

In a simple example, a miller may buy wheat that is to be converted into flour. At the same time, the miller will contract to sell an equal amount of wheat, which the miller does not presently own, to another trader. The miller agrees to deliver the second lot of wheat at the time the flour is ready for market and at the price current at the time of the agreement. If the price of wheat declined during the period between the miller's purchase of the grain and the flour's entrance onto the market, there will also be a resulting drop in the price of flour. That loss must be sustained by the miller. However, since the miller has a contract to sell wheat at the older, higher price, the miller makes up for this loss on the flour sale by the gain on the wheat sale. Hedging is also employed by stock and bond traders, export-import traders, and some manufacturers. [19]

HEDGE FUND:

A hedge fund is a highly speculative, largely unregulated investment device that is typically open to a limited range of investors who pay a performance fee to the fund's investment manager. Every hedge fund has its own investment strategy that determines the type of investments it undertakes and these strategies are highly individual. They undertake a wider range of investment and trading activities than traditional investment funds, and invest in a broader range of assets. As the name implies, hedge funds often seek to hedge some of the risks inherent in their investments using a variety of methods, notably short selling and derivatives.

Most hedge funds are open only to a limited range of professional or wealthy investors who meet criteria set by regulators, and are accordingly exempted from many of the regulations that govern ordinary investment funds. They came to public view in 1998 when Long-Term Capital Management nearly collapsed, requiring a $3.5 billion bailout organized by the Federal Reserve Bank of New York and paid by private banks. The bailout led to a number of investigations into hedge funds and a call for greater regulation and scrutiny.

FUTURES:CONTRACT

A futures contract is a standardized contract between two parties to buy or sell a specified asset of standardized quantity and quality at a specified future date at a price agreed today. The contracts are traded on a futures exchange. They are not direct securities like stocks, bonds, rights or warrants, but are still securities. The price is determined by the instantaneous equilibrium between the forces of supply and demand among competing buy and sell orders on the exchange at the time of purchase or sale of the contract. [20]

In many cases, the underlying asset to a futures contract may not be traditional commodities but could be currencies, securities of financial instruments and intangible assets or reference items such as stock indexes and interest rates.

OPTIONS

"An option is a derivative instrument that establishes a contract between two parties concerning the buying or selling of an asset at a reference price. The buyer of the option gains the right, but not the obligation, to engage in some specific transaction on the asset, while the seller incurs the obligation to fulfill the transaction if so requested by the buyer. The price of an option derives from the difference between the reference price and the value of the underlying asset plus a premium based on the time remaining until the expiration of the option.'

"An option which conveys the right to buy something is called a "call"; an option which conveys the right to sell is called a "put". The reference price at which the underlying may be traded is called the 'exercise price". The process of activating an option is referred to as "exercising" it. Most options have an expiration date. If the option is not exercised by the expiration date, it becomes void and worthless.'

"In return for granting the option, the originator collects a payment, the "premium" from the buyer. The writer of an option must make good on delivering (or receiving) the underlying asset or its cash equivalent, if the option is exercised.'

"An option can usually be sold by its original buyer to another party. Many are traded on an exchange among the general public, while other over-the-counter options are customized on an ad hoc basis, usually by an investment bank." [21]

CREDIT DEFAULT SWAP

A credit default swap (CDS) is a credit derivative contract between two counterparties. It can be almost thought of as a form of insurance. If a borrower of money does not repay his loan, he "defaults." If a lender has purchased a CDS on that loan from an insurance company, the lender can then use the default as a credit to swap it in exchange for a repayment from an insurance company. However, one does not need to be the lender to profit from this situation. Anyone can purchase a CDS. If a borrower does not repay his loan on time and defaults, not only does the lender get paid by the insurance company, but the speculator gets paid as well. It is in the lender's best interest that he gets his money back, either from the borrower, or from the insurance company if the borrower is unable to pay back his loan. However, it is in the speculator's best interest that the borrower never repays his loan and defaults because that is the only way that the speculator can then take that default, turn it into a credit, and swap it for a cash payment from an insurance company.

Credit default swaps have existed since the early 1990s, but the market increased tremendously starting in 2003. By the end of 2007, the outstanding amount was $62 trillion, falling to $38 trillion by the end of 2008 as the financial crisis unraveled. [22]

During the congressional debate in the aftermath of the 2007 crisis, "few questioned the need for more regulation; but freewheeling swaps markets were not the main cause even though they played an unwelcome role, multiplying and masking leverage. End-user firms -- from airlines to brewers that use swaps to hedge risk -- worry that their costs will rise. Big dealers, such as JPMorgan Chase and Goldman Sachs, moan that there will be unintended consequences. American bank-holding companies that use swaps as a 'cash cow' made $12.2 billion from derivatives trading in the third quarter of last year." [23]

The regulation of derivatives remains an open question for Congress. "Treasury Secretary Geithner is in a difficult spot. Last year, as Congress was negotiating what became the Dodd-Frank Financial-Reform law, he sought to exclude foreign exchange derivatives from new regulations. After debate, Congress split the difference by including currencies but also giving Geithner the authority to study the instruments and decide whether to exempt them." [24]

Derivatives in their various forms were high-profile financial tools (instruments) that became one of the drivers leading up to the financial bubble that got bust in the 2007 financial meltdown. Let's fit them into the story of that financial crisis as it is discussed in the following chapter.

SEVENTEEN: 2007 FINANCIAL MELTDOWN

In 2007, our nation encountered the worse financial crisis since the 1930's Great Depression. It resulted in the "collapse of large financial institutions, the bailout of banks by national governments, and downturns in stock markets around the world ... The housing market also suffered resulting in numerous foreclosures ... it contributed to the failure of key businesses, declines in consumer wealth estimated in trillions of U.S. dollars, substantial financial commitment increases by governments, and a significant decline in economic activity." [25]

The causes will be debated by economists and historians for decades, but causes have already been suggested by experts who attribute them to such things as the following:

Deregulation of business activity.

Growth of a housing bubble.

Easy credit.

Weak and fraudulent underwriting practice.

Subprime lending.

Predatory lending.

Increased debt burden and over-leveraging.

Financial innovation and complexity.

Incorrect pricing of risk.

Boom and collapse of the shadow banking system.

Systemic breaches in accountability and ethics at all levels.

Two things that occurred simultaneously were triggering events: a liquidity shortfall in the U.S. banking system, and the bursting of the housing bubble. As unemployment began to rise, many homeowners could not meet mortgage payments and default rates began to increase quickly thereafter. Then a cascading began that ended in a meltdown of our nation's financial system that spread to the global economy.

In a financial collapse of this magnitude, there likely would be a number of contributing causes that are inter-linked and a synergy among these that fed off the weaknesses of each other. The following paragraphs discuss individually each of the causes that have been identified.

DEREGULATION:

As discussed earlier in the chapter on Monetary Policy, there are two competing economic philosophies: Keynesian and Free Market. All Republican and Democratic administrations operated essentially with Keynesian from 1944 until 1975, when President Ford in a speech to a business audience promised, "I will take the shackles off American businessmen and get the federal government out of your business, out of your lives, out of your pocketbook, and out of your hair as possibly I can." That was the point at which the U.S. government adopted de-regulation policies and changed to a Free Market approach, which was followed by all administrations until the meltdown and enactment late in 2008 of the TARP program by the Bush administration.

Following behind Ford's deregulation initiative in 1975, came a series of similar actions by the subsequent presidents from both parties. Jimmy Carter's *Depository Institution Deregulation and Monetary Control Act of 1980* phased out a number of restrictions on banks' financial practices. In 1982, President Reagan signed the *Garn-St. Germaine Deposit Instability Act* that continued the process of bank deregulation. In 1999, President Clinton signed the *Gram-Leach-Bliley Act* that repealed the *Glass-Steagall Act* and this reduced the separation between commercial banks and investment banks. In 2004 under President Bush, the SEC (Securities and Exchange Commission) relaxed the capital rules, which enabled investment banks to increase their level of debt. As early as 1977, Fed Chairman Alan Greenspan fought to keep the derivatives market unregulated. During his long tenure as Chairman of the Federal Reserve, he was an out-spoken champion of deregulation of our nation's banking and financial system.

Within the context of all these moves, the U.S. financial system moved dramatically in the thirty years prior to the meltdown to a Free Market economy with little regulation over commercial banks, investment banks, and other financial institutions. A *Lazzie Faire* atmosphere developed during this climate of "anything goes." A Free Market depends on self-policing and counter-balancing of economic variables to maintain reasonable stability. As stated in an earlier chapter, Alan Greenspan said in hindsight after the meltdown in testimony before Congress, "I always thought that in a Free-Market economy, it would be essentially self-policing, but I now see no alternative to the imposition of regulation over the institutions of our financial systems."

GROWTH OF THE HOUSING BUBBLE:

"The price of the typical American home increased by 124% between 1997 and 2006, and the median home price rose to 4 times the median household income." [26] That is a formula for a housing disaster, which occurred when unemployment suddenly increased and millions could no longer pay their mortgage bills. Even those with jobs could not refinance to avoid the higher payments with adjustable-rate mortgages that suddenly became effective. By mid-2009, fifteen percent of all mortgages were delinquent or in default. By 2011 with the decline in house prices, fifty percent of American homes were under-water with their mortgage debt greater than the sales value of their home.

EASY CREDIT:

Lower interest rates encourage borrowing. During the three years prior to 2003, the Federal Reserve lowered the Federal Funds rate from 6.5% to 1%. Large amounts of foreign funds flowed into the U.S. to finance its imports. This "flood" of liquidity created a demand for various kinds of financial assets, and obtaining credit was easy for a new home or expansion in the business community.

Then between 2004 and 2006, the Fed raised the Federal Funds rate significantly, which caused an increase in adjustable-rate mortgages, making them more expensive for homeowners. This contributed to deflating the housing bubble. The USA housing and financial assets declined dramatically in value as a result.

WEAK AND FRAUDLENT UNDERWRITING PRACTICES:

In testimony before congress, one of the country's leading underwriting experts stated that the collapse of mortgage underwriting standards became endemic. His testimony states "by 2006, 60% of mortgages purchased by the banking group, Citi, from 1600 mortgage companies were defective (not underwritten to policy, or did not contain all policy documentation)." [27] This meant that the analytical process of performing a fiduciary duty for the mortgage industry was missing-in-action, with the predictable result that the entire housing market was resting on a bed of quicksand.

"Subprime mortgages were 10% of all mortgages until 2004, when they spiked to nearly 20%. At the same time, the SEC relaxed the net capital rule, which allowed banks to increase their financial leverage and aggressively expand their insurance of mortgage-backed securities. This applied competitive pressure on Fannie Mae and Freddie Mac to expand their riskier lending. By early 2008, subprime mortgage delinquency rates reached 25%." [28]

PREDATORY LENDING

Predatory lending refers to the practice of unscrupulous lenders enticing borrowers to enter into "unsound" loans for inappropriate purposes. A classic bait-and-switch method was used by Countrywide Financial that advertised low interest rate for home financing. These loans were written into contracts and swapped for more expensive products on the day of closing. Whereas the advertisement might state a 1.5% interest rate, the consumer would be put into an adjustable rate mortgage." [29]

INCREASED DEBT BURDEN OR OVER-LEDGERING

American households, financial institutions, and government enterprises all increased their debt burden or over-leveraged in the years preceding the meltdown. This increased their vulnerability to the collapse of the housing bubble and worsened the ensuing economic downturn. Here are some sobering statistics.

U.S. home mortgage debt relative to GDP increased from an average of 46% during the 1990s to 73% during 2008, reaching 10.5 trillion.

U.S. private debt in 1981 was 123% of GDP; by the third quarter of 2008, it was 290%.

The top five investment banks in 2004-2007 each significantly increased their financial leverage to about 30% of GDP. This increased their vulnerability to a financial shock. During the meltdown, Lehman Brothers was liquidated, Bear Sterns and Merrill Lynch were sold at fire-sale prices, and Goldman Sach and Morgan Stanley became commercial banks that involuntarily subjected themselves to more stringent regulation in the future. Fannie Mae and Freddie Mac, two government sponsored enterprises, were placed into conservatorship by the U.S. Government in 2008. [30]

These seven latter entities were highly leveraged and had $9 trillion in debt or guaranteed obligations; yet they were not subject to the same regulations as depository banks.

FINANCIAL INNOVATION AND COMPLEXITY

The term innovation refers to the development by the financial community of new things to sell or to assist them in obtaining financing. Examples of such innovations were the following: [31]

Adjustable-rate mortgages.

Bundling of subprime mortgages into mortgage-backed securities.

Collateralized debt obligations (CDO) for sale to investors.

Credit default swaps (CDS).

The rise of derivatives and these products expanded dramatically in the years leading up to the crisis. They vary in complexity and also in the ease with which then can be valued on the books of financial institutions. For example, "Collateralized debt obligations (CDO) grew from $20 billion in Q1 2004 to its peak of over $180 billion by Q1 2007, and then declined back under $20 billion by Q1 2008. In the stable of (CDO) was a portfolio called synthetic CDO that enabled a theoretically infinite amount to be wagered on the finite value of housing loans outstanding, provided that buyers and sellers of derivatives could be found. Those kinds of things were complex and not easily understood by the general public nor in some instances even by the investment community." [32]

A government regulator wrote in 2009 that "certain financial innovations enabled firms to circumvent regulations, such as off-balance sheet financing that affects the leverage or capital cushion reported by major banks, stating: 'an enormous part of what banks did in the early part of this decade -- the off-balance-sheet vehicles, the derivatives and the shadow banking system itself -- was to find a way around regulation.' " [33]

INCORRECT PRICING OF RISK

"The pricing of risk refers to the incremental compensation required by investors for taking on additional risk, which may be measured by interest rates or fees. For a variety of reasons, market participants did not accurately measure the risk inherent with financial innovation such as MBS and CDO's or understand its impact on the overall stability of the financial system." [34] During the crisis and in its aftermath, many of the high risk products were simply liquidated while the recovery rate for others, such as collateralized debt obligations (CDO) was 32 cents on the dollar.

"One of the more extreme examples of incorrect pricing of risk was by American Insurance Group (AIG), which insured obligations of financial institutions through the usage of credit default swaps (CDS). The transactions involved AIG receiving a premium in exchange for a promise to pay a premium to party A in the event party B defaulted. However, AIG did not have the financial strength to support its many commitments as the crisis progressed and was taken over by the government in September 2008." [35]

As financial assets became more complex, the pricing and value placed on risk became harder and harder to assess. Authorities could no longer calculate the risks and started relying on the assessments of the institutions themselves. At the same time, the rating agencies had already virtually abdicated their fiduciary responsibility for risk assessment.

To further complicate risk assessment, there was a conflict of interest between professional investment managers and their institutional clients, because the managers were compensated based on the volume of assets of the clients that gave an incentive for them to expand assets. Many chose to continue to invest client funds in over-priced and riskier investments.

As discussed in earlier chapters, all investments have a trade-off between the risks involved and the potential return. Many professionals in the financial community forgot this basic principle and failed to understand that their investments with high potential returns involved risks far beyond any they had ever previously encountered.

BOOM AND COLLAPSE OF THE SHADOW BANKING SYSTEM

The shadow banking system consists of non-depository banks and other financial entities such as investment banks, hedge funds, and money market funds. These grew in size to nearly equal the importance of the traditional commercial banking sector in the critical role of lending business the money necessary to operate. The shadow banking system had combined assets of $10 trillion, and this equaled the total assets of the entire traditional depository banking system of $10 trillion.

According to Timothy Geithner, who became Secretary of the Treasury in 2009, a significant part of blame for the freezing of credit markets was a "run" on this "parallel" banking system when investors stopped providing funds to many entities in the system. Paul Krugman, laureate of the Nobel Prize in economics, described the run on the shadow banking system as the "core of what happened" to cause the crisis. He referred to this lack of control as "malign neglect" and argued that regulation should have been imposed on the banking-like activity. [36]

The security markets supported by the shadow banking system nearly shut down during the crisis and this caused further turmoil in the aftermath. According to the Brookings Institution, the traditional banking system did not have the capital to close the gap; so it would take a number of years of strong profits to generate sufficient capital to support the additional lending volume needed by American business.

SYSTEMIC BREACHES IN ACCOUNTABILITY AND ETHICS

Steadily decreasing interest rates backed by the Federal Reserve for 25 years prior to the 2007 crisis created easy credit conditions, fueling a housing construction boom, and encouraging debt-financed consumption. In an atmosphere of *Lazzie Faire*, few felt there would be accountability for their actions. The combination of easy credit and excess liquidity contributed to a housing bubble, loans of various types (mortgage, credit card, and auto) were easy to obtain, and as a result, consumers assumed an unprecedented debt load.

Innovation in financial markets created new investment instruments of high risk that found ways around traditional regulatory controls. These sometimes employed marginal ethics or predatory schemes such as a bait-and-switch tactics utilized to sell mortgages to naïve home buyers. The combination of all these factors created systemic breaches in accountability at all levels, and these were often accompanied by lapses of ethical standards.

When this vulnerable system encountered the triggering events of unemployment and mortgage defaults, the entire system began to cascade down like a house of cards.

A GLOBAL CRISIS

The crisis in the United States rapidly spread into a global economic shock, resulting in a number of European bank failures, decline in over-sea stock indexes, and reduction in the market value of global equities and commodities. Derivatives, MBS (mortgage backed securities), and CDO (credit default swaps) had also been purchased by corporate and institutional investors globally, which increased linkage between large financial institutions.

World political leaders coordinated efforts to reduce fears, but the crisis continued. At the end of 2008, a global currency crisis developed with investors transferring vast capital resources into stronger currencies such as the dollar, yen, and Swiss franc, leading many emergent economies to seek aid from the IMF (International Monetary Fund).

Some developing countries that had seen economic growth now saw significant slowdowns. The Brooking Institution reported that U.S. consumption accounted for more than a third of the growth in global consumption, and the rest of the world depended on the U.S. consumer as a source for global demand. With a recession in the United States, declines in world-wide growth elsewhere were dramatic.

SUMMARY

The United States has encountered two major financial meltdowns during the past century: the Great Depression of the 1930's, and the financial crisis of 2007. A financial collapse of our capitalist economic system of such magnitude must be addressed by a look at the basic philosophies of economic theory. We have utilized principally two of these over the past century: Free Market and Keynesian. A Free Market is a market in which there is little or no economic intervention and regulation by the government except to enforce taxes, private contracts, and ownership of property. Keynesian philosophy advocates active policy responses by the public sector, including monetary policy action by the central bank and fiscal policy action by the government to stabilize output over the business cycle.

From the 1930's until 1975, all Republican and Democratic administrations employed what was essentially the Keynesian philosophy with considerable pragmatic modifications from time-to-time. This was an era of general financial stability, but low corporate profits and slow economic growth. Then in 1975, there was a deliberate change to the Free Market deregulation philosophy throughout nearly all sectors of the nation's economy.

During these decades of de-regulation leading up to the meltdown, a climate of *lassie faire* developed in the housing, banking and financial communities that left them increasingly vulnerable to the disaster that ultimately occurred. Like a ticking time-bomb, the finances of these institutions exploded when the fuse reached the triggering event -- bursting of the housing bubble. In the aftermath of the meltdown, trillions of wealth became lost to Americans.

EIGHTEEN :
BOOKKEEPING AND RECORDS

A serious mistake I made early in my investment activities was to fail to maintain adequate bookkeeping records. This hampered me in a number of ways:

My forecast of an investment strategy was difficult because I could not look back at my past historical record.

I could not evaluate the performance of individual investments without the entry level time and amounts.

I had no record of the initial amount of an individual investment; therefore, I was unable to determine "basis points;" and was unable to accurately calculate capital gains for my IRS tax report.

These were major problems when it came income tax time. I have since developed a minimal bookkeeping system that is adequate, yet not time consuming. It consists of the following:

Journal: that records every transaction involving my investments, income tax, and other major personal expenditures and income transactions.

Investment Summary: this Excel spreadsheet provides a record of all my current investment assets. I would not know what was in my portfolio without it.

Net Worth statement: this provides my financial status on an annual basis. It helps me maintain an investment perspective.

Analysis and strategy: On at least a semiannual basis, I conduct an appraisal of my investment results and develop a strategy for the future.

JOURNAL: Every investment transaction and other major financial transactions such as income tax should be recorded chronologically in the journal together with supporting information.

Date	Transaction	Debit	Credit
2/1/10	USAA Growth fund	3,000	
	Wells Fargo checking acct.		3,000
	Purchase IRA Growth Fund 150share @ $ 20/sh. Confirmation# 2300236		
2/7/10	Fidelity Puritan Fund	1,500	
	Fidelity Money Market fund	1000	
	Fidelity Magellan Fund		2,500
	IRA transfer from Magellan Fund into Money Market and Puritan fund. Confirmation # 4600078		
2/9/10	USAA Growth Fund	2,000	
	Wells Fargo Savings acct		2,000
	Initial investment in a non-IRA USAA Growth Fund. This becomes my "basis points". Confirmation # 2300478		
3/20/10	Vanguard money market	5000	
	Wells Fargo savings		5000
	Took IRA distribution from Vanguard No federal tax was withheld. My YTD IRA distributions now total $8000. Confirmation # 45955		
6/15/10	Internal Revenue Service	1800	
	Well Fargo Savings acct.		1800
	Paid 1st quarter pre-payment to IRS My YTD prepayments are now $1800		

INVESTMENT SUMMARY

Asset	1/1/2010		6/30/2010	
	Value	Portfolio	Value	Portfolio
W.F.	25000	25000	20000	20000
USAA				
Mny. Mkt.	25600		22000	
Corner-s	1000		500	
		26600		22500
Vanguard.				
mny. mkt	8500		8200	
Winsor	3000		1500	
		11500		9700
IRA INVEST. TOTAL	63100		52200	

NET WORTH STATEMENT

Assets::
    Personal Assets:

	Home	$ XXX
	Personal Property	XXX
	Bank checking	XXX
	Bank Savings	XXX
	Sub Total	$ XXX
Investment Assets:		$XXX
	Total Assets:	$ XXXX

Liabilities:
    Mortgage: $ XXX
                  Total Liabilities $ XXXX

Net Worth   .... $ XXXXX

APPRAISAL AND STRATEGY ANALYSIS: It is important to conduct

periodic appraisals of your investments and develop an investment strategy. This can be accomplished informally, or more formally as I do.

An example of my approach is in Appendix C, which has the analysis I conducted on 4/27/2010. I do this at least semi-annually and more often if major changes have occurred. I deliberately vary my approach to keep thinking fresh, but I always address the basics.

NINTEEN:
PRINCIPLES FOR INVESTING

We Americans are a contrary lot. For example, where do we look for investment advice? I began thinking about this as the result of a recent study concerning our use of vitamin supplements, which found that one-third of American adults take vitamins. This is despite the use of vitamins has been pooh-poohed by most doctors, the American Medical Association, and the American Dietetic Association. Isn't it amazing that so many of us agree on something and subject ourselves to daily pill popping, all the while thumbing our noses at the experts? The Surgeon General trying to promote the use of vitamins would struggle to get half of us to use them. Whose advice will we accept?

It was within this context that I decided to give investment advice. My credentials are as good as any vitamin store clerk. I'm not an economist, but I gained some "street smarts" from a long career as a business executive. I read, listen, and learn; I am wise enough to know what I do not know. I have also been successful, living quite comfortably off my investments and watching my net worth almost double (with some financial income from consulting) during the twenty years of my retirement.

Very early in the process I learned the importance of having some simple principles to guide my investment strategies so I did not have to start from "ground zero" every day. These are the ground rules I keep coming back to for assurance that I'm still on track. I obtained these from investment experts and then put them in a form I could understand and use.

(#1) <u>Know the Market</u>: Have an understanding of the basics that drive investments. Recognize that changes will occur in the future, what the causes might be, and the possible effect on my investments. If I can't describe these things in simple language, then I don't yet understand them.

(#2) <u>Know My Resources</u>: Have a clear understanding of what financial resources I have available.

(#3) <u>Have An Investment Strategy</u>: Develop my objectives; then a plan for how I intend to invest, and within this game plan include how I will react to change.

(#4) <u>Understand My Investments</u>: Invest only in things I fully understand. For example: I do not have an adequate understanding of bonds; so I avoid these until I learn more about them.

(#5) <u>Have a Termination Action Plan</u>: Never invest in anything unless I understand under what circumstances and how I may terminate the investment.

(#6) <u>Set Up Accurate Accounting</u>: I must maintain accurate records to keep abreast of all investment transactions, particularly those involving the IRS.

(#7) <u>Analyze Results</u>: I should conduct an in-depth review of each investment on at least a semiannual basis, reach conclusions regarding the degree of success or failure of each, and of the overall investment strategy.

(#8) <u>Maintain Perspective</u>: I must not be overly influenced by market changes or the appraisal by economic gurus; rather I must follow my strategy and react with changes in accordance with the game plan. If the strategy needs modification, then change it and act; but do this intelligently without great emotion; and do not overreact to day-to-day events. I must recognize that over a period of years my investments will encounter market's ups and downs, and the strategy must allow provisions for this.

(#9) <u>Learn and Grow</u>: I must constantly seek to improve my abilities by reading, asking the right questions, and learning to listen.

(#10) <u>Be Decisive -- Action</u>: I must remember that I manage my investments and must control my own destiny. When the time for a decision is at hand, I must act on the basis of the best information available and, right or wrong; get on with the ball game. Never accept the paralysis of indecision. Within this context I must also recognize that the correct decision at any given time may be to do nothing -- that sometimes is the most decisive action of all. I must have the courage to act, or not to act, whether it is to charge ahead or to stand and hold the fort.

I must convert these ten principles into action for them to have any value. These principles for managing my investments have served me quite well for a number of years, and yes, I do also take vitamins.

TWENTY: SUMMARY

Before I begin to read a book or magazine article, I first review the credentials of the author, because that will reveal something about their qualifications, biases, and credibility to discuss their subject. Within that context, let me review my own background so you can make the same assessment about what has been contained in this book. I did not do that up-front, because too much personal information is often a turn-off.

After obtaining university degrees, and three years as a naval officer, I began a 30 year career as an executive in a multi-national company, the world's largest producer of packaging and glass products (Owens-Illinois Inc). For a decade I was their Corporate Manager of Quality Assurance. After retirement, I continued to provide consulting services on a part-time basis to their world-wide affiliates. After an extensive study of economics and how to invest in the stock market, I wrote a book about what I had learned. The experience served me well, because my net worth doubled during the fifteen years since then. Now, on to the summary.

The stock market is a pawn of the economy: it becomes either the beneficiary or the victim; therefore, a wise investor will understand economics. It involves the needs of people and their resources, and is personal because needs spring from the gut and we deal with them by using the resources we have.

Five parameters play the major role in causing the stock market to move up or down. These are:
CORPORATE EARNINGS
INTEREST RATES
INFLATION
LIQUIDITY

DOLLAR EXCHANGE RATE

Inflation is the most immediate causative factor. Governments attempt to follow fiscal and monetary policies that maintain economic stability, and inflation is a bogey that intervenes in the business cycle as it surges between boom and bust.

Other secondary factors affect the stock market, such as GDP, unemployment, and the federal deficit. They should be evaluated on how they impact the five primary parameters.

Where to invest? There are many options such as: 401(k)'s, IRA's, annuities, certificates of deposit (CD's), bonds, real estate, bank savings accounts, mutual funds, and equity stock. Mutual Funds are excellent investments because they have advantages such as: diversification, ease of investing, dollar cost averaging, good management costs, and investing expertise.

With any investment there is always a trade-off between the degree-of-risk and potential rate-of-return. An investor should remember this and make choices based on their individual needs and comfort zone in dealing with the ups-and-downs of the stock market.

The stock exchange is a rough bartering arena that involves a buyer and a seller where each is motivated by their own needs -- the process involves fear and greed. This creates an unstable climate where the naive or uninformed investor must proceed with caution, or stay out. Fortunes can be slowly made and quickly lost.

The United States has encountered two major financial meltdowns during the past century: the Great Depression of the 1930's, and the recent Financial Crisis of 2007. After the financial collapse of our capitalist system of such magnitude, we should look at the philosophies of economic theory. We have utilized two of these: Free Market and Keynesian. In a Free Market there is little economic intervention and regulation by the state except to enforce taxes, private contracts, and ownership of property. In the Keynesian Market, the Federal Reserve Bank, Administration, and Congress intervene using monetary and fiscal policies to stabilize the business cycle.

All United States Administrations employed the Keynesian philosophy from the 1930's until 1975. There was a change to the Free Market philosophy at that time, which began with deregulation in many sectors of the economy. With the TARP program late in 2008, the Bush administration brought an abrupt, Keynesian modification. In the absence of new laws governing market regulation, we have essentially returned to a Free Market economy.

The meltdown of 2007 was the worse financial crisis since the Great Depression. It resulted in the collapse of financial institutions, bailout of banks by the government, collapse of a housing bubble, and a decline in consumer wealth estimated in the $ trillions. The triggering event was an increase in unemployment, which led to an epidemic of mortgage defaults. A financial meltdown of this magnitude had numerous inter-linked causes -- a dozen of these have been identified.

The crisis in the United States rapidly spread into a global economic shock. Now several years in its aftermath, only minimal measures have been enacted to prevent a reoccurrence, and our economies remain vulnerable to the two competing rivals -- degree of risk and potential rate of return. A wise investor will remember this.

Within the financial jungle of the economy and stock market, how is an investor to proceed? Ten investment principles I have successfully followed during the past two decades are listed in a latter chapter.

The final conclusion to take from this book is: if you want to be successful in investing, you'd better understand economics.

APPENDICE:

APPENDIX A: BIBLIOGRAPHY

Adam Smith, *An Inquiry into the Nature and Causes of the Wealth of Nations*, 1977

John Maynard Keynes, *The General Theory of Employment, Interest, and Money*, 1935

Alan Greenspan, *The Age of Turbulence*, Penguin Press, New York, NY, 1970

Martin Feldstein, *A National Bureau of Economic Research Council*, University of Chicago Press, 1988

Volcker, Gyohten, *Changing Fortunes*, Times Books, 1992

Dornbusch, *Macro-Economics*, McGraw Hill, 1984

Heilbroner, *The Worldly Philosophers*, Simon & Schuster, 1986

Harvey, *Modern Economics*, Macmillan, 5th Ed. 1988

Ellis, *Investment Policy*, Business One Irwin, 1993

Stein, Foss, *An Illustrated Guide to the American Economy*, AEI Press, 1992

Ammer, Christine, *The A to Z of Investing*, A Mentor Book of New American Library, 1986

Colliers Encyclopedia, *Banking Systems*, Vol 3, 34D-34J, 1960

Wikipedia, *The Free Encyclopedia*, Internet 2011

Downes, John, *Dictionary of Finance and Investment Terms*, Barron's Educational Series, Inc., 1985.

APPENDIX B 30 YEAR ECONOMIC STATISTICS

	S&P INDEX	EARN/ SHARE	PE RATIO	3 Mo T Bill	INFL	GDP	UNEMP
1980	104	13	8	19	12.5	-0.2	7
1981	105	12.3	8.5	18	8.9	-0.1	7.5
1982	150	14.6	10.3	13	3.8	-1.1	9.5
1983	165	13.5	12.2	8.4	3.8	6.7	9.5
1984	165	16.3	10.1	10.5	3.9	4.5	7.4
1985	210	15.2	13.8	8	3.8	3.3	7.1
1986	242	14.5	16.7	5.5	1.1	2.2	6.9
1987	247	19.9	12.4	5.8	4.4	4.5	6.1
1988	277	24.1	11.5	7	4.4	3.3	5.4
1989	353	24.3	14.5	8	4.6	1.6	5.2
1990	330	22.6	14.6	7.5	6.1	0.2	5.6
1991	417	19.3	21.6	5.1	3.1	0.3	6.8
1992	436	20.9	20.9	3.3	2.9	3.9	7.5
1993	466	26.9	17.3	3.1	2.7	3.3	6.9
1994	461	31.75	14.5	5.5	2.9	4	6.1
1995	602	37.7	16.3	5	2.5	0.5	5.6
1996	741	40.6	18.2	5	3.3	4.3	5.4
1997	970	44	22.1	5.2	1.8	3.9	4.9
1998	1229	44.3	27.8	4.4	1.5	6.1	4.5
1999	1469	51.7	28.4	5.4	3	5	4.2
2000	1320	56.1	23.5	5.8	3.5	3.7	4
2001	1148	38.85	29.6	3.5	2.5	0.8	4.7
2002	880	46	19.1	1.6	1.6	1.6	5.8
2003	1108	54.7	20.3	1	2.3	2.5	6
2004	1212	67.7	17.9	1.4	2.7	3.9	5.5
2005	1248	76.5	16.3	4	3.4	3.2	5.1
2006	1418	87.7	16.2	4.9	3.2	3.3	4.6
2007	1468	92	15.9	3.2	2.9	2.5	5
2008	903	82.5	10.9	0.4	0.1	-5.4	6.2
2009	1115	56.9	19.6	1.5	2.1	5.9	10.1
2010	1260	77.3	16.3	1.8	1.6	2.9	9

APPENDIX C: FEDERAL RESERVE FOMC MINUTES

The Federal Open Market Committee meeting is held every six weeks. They determine the overall monetary policy, set targets, and decide what sort of tactics will be used in open market transactions. The minutes are kept as highly guarded secrets for weeks after the meeting to avoid counter-moves which would make the tactics less effective. The following is a press release issued on January 26, 2011 several weeks after the previous FOMC meeting.

FEDERAL RESERVE press release

Release Date: January 26, 2011
　　　　　1. For immediate release

Information received since the Federal Open Market Committee met in December confirms that the economic recovery is continuing, though at a rate that has been insufficient to bring about a significant improvement in labor market conditions. Growth in household spending picked up late last year, but remains constrained by high unemployment, modest income growth, lower housing wealth, and tight credit. Business spending on equipment and software is rising, while investment in nonresidential structures is still weak. Employers remain reluctant to add to payrolls. The housing sector continues to be depressed. Although commodity prices have risen, longer-term inflation expectations have remained stable, and measures of underlying inflation have been trending downward.

Consistent with its statutory mandate, the Committee seeks to foster maximum employment and price stability. Currently, the unemployment rate is elevated, and measures of underlying inflation are somewhat low, relative to levels that the Committee judges to be consistent, over the longer run, with its dual mandate. Although the Committee anticipates a gradual return to higher levels of resource utilization in a context of price stability, progress toward its objectives has been disappointingly slow.

To promote a stronger pace of economic recovery and to help ensure that inflation, over time, is at levels consistent with its mandate, the Committee decided today to continue expanding its holdings of securities as announced in November. In particular, the Committee is maintaining its existing policy of reinvesting principal payments from its securities holdings and intends to purchase $600 billion of longer-term Treasury securities by the end of the second quarter of 2011. The Committee will regularly review the pace of its securities purchases and the overall size of the asset-purchase program in light of incoming information and will adjust the program as needed to best foster maximum employment and price stability.

The Committee will maintain the target range for the federal funds rate at 0 to 1/4 percent and continues to anticipate that economic conditions, including low rates of resource utilization, subdued inflation trends, and stable inflation expectations, are likely to warrant exceptionally low levels for the federal funds rate for an extended period.

The Committee will continue to monitor the economic outlook and financial developments and will employ its policy tools as necessary to support the economic recovery and to help ensure that inflation, over time, is at levels consistent with its mandate.

Voting for the FOMC monetary policy action were: Ben S. Bernanke, Chairman; William C. Dudley, Vice Chairman; Elizabeth A. Duke; Charles L. Evans; Richard W. Fisher; Narayana Kocherlakota; Charles I. Plosser; Sarah Bloom Raskin; Daniel K. Tarullo; Kevin M. Warsh; and Janet L. Yellen.

APPENDIX C: APPRAISAL AND STRATEGY

The following is an economic analysis I made on 4/27/2010:

ECONOMIC ANALYSIS

On my last economic analysis two months ago on 2/20/10, my portfolio contained 35% in equities with the remainder in annuities, CD's, and money market. I concluded that the bull market would continue and gain about 8% prior to the end of the year. At the time the S&P 500 index was at 1109, so my estimate was a rise to 1194.

I will again discuss the interlinked parameters of the political climate, the economy, and the stock market.

Political Climate:

Not much change. The Obama Administration remains in control despite the entrenchment of the Republican minority who are sitting on the sidelines. The gridlock effect on the market is minor, but the long term effect is difficult to predict. Regardless, history does not suggest a stock market negative in a mid-year election.

The Economy:

We are coming out of the financial meltdown and recession faster than anyone predicted thanks to Bush, Paulson, and Bernanke with their TARP, and Bush, Geithner, and Bernanke with their Stimulus Bill. All signs point to continued recovery.

The end of the year S&P 500 Index was at 1115. The 3 mo. T Bill rate is 1.8%, reflecting the continued low interest rates, and inflation remains low at 2.1%. Neither of them is predicted to rise in the near term. However the unemployment rate remains high at 9.7% and is unlikely to go down appreciably during the coming year, because of the historic time lag between an economic recovery and growing new jobs.

Current GDP numbers are not available but predictions are 3-4%. YTD. Cumulative corporate earnings are currently estimated at $64/share giving a P/E of 17.4, which seems a reasonable valuation, and earnings are expected to rise to $77/share by year end.

Unemployment continues at 9.7%, and will remain high well into 2011 and probably beyond. That is having little effect on the stock market and is more of a political issue -- unless someone in your family is unemployed, and then it is a very personal issue.

The Stock Market::

Let's do some "what ifs."

If cumulated corporate earnings are at $77/share as predicted for end of the year, and Investors are comfortable with the current P/E of 17.4 the Index will be at 1339.

If investor optimism in the present rate of recover causes a rise in the P/E to 19, the market will rise to 1463.

If investor psychology moves to its P/E long term historical average of 15.4, then the year end Index will be exactly where it ended today at 1185.

Who knows? Investors seem to be currently optimistic. However, I expect to see investor psychology move the P/E ratio toward its 50 year historical average of 15.5, but perhaps not all the way down. There are several possible risks ahead:

Default problems with Greece and Portugal.

The Fed could raise interest rates if inflation rears its head.

The deficit is certainly an issue.

Summary and Strategy::

I am a nervous investor in turbulent times; however, I expect the market to remain reasonable stable, and my strategy will be to remain with my current portfolio.

Bernie Keating

ENDNOTES

1. Adam Smith, *An Inquiry Into the Nature and Causes of the Wealth of Nations, 1776* In this book, Smith explained that the fragments of social activity fitted together into a cohesive whole. The result was a blueprint for a new philosophy called economics. His theory led to a doctrine of "Laissez Faire." To him, the least government is best; all governments are spendthrift, irresponsible and unproductive. Some still argue this today. He was the ultimate proponent of the "Free Market."

2. John Maynard Keynes, a Cambridge professor, was an economist during the period between the two World Wars. In 1935 he published *The General Theory of Employment, Interest, and Money*, which argues that the business cycle in the economy could stand still in a depression like a ship becalmed, and might need a nudge from government to get moving again. The pros and cons of the Keynesian theory are still being debated.

3. Price Earnings Ratio. The relationship between earnings and the price of stock is expressed as a ratio, Price/Earnings (P/E). This number has meaning only in a historical context. Over the last 50 years, the ratio has averaged 15.5. When the ratio falls lower than this, it suggests investors are bearish and are being cautious. It seldom goes as low as 10, even in hard times. When the ratio moves above its average, it is an indication investors are bullish and are willing to pay an additional increment for stock. Whenever it reaches 20 beware, because

the stock market has moved up into a speculative range. During the past decade, the P/E was often above 20, even up to 30, suggesting a highly speculative market. We know what happened to that market in 2008.

4. Alan Greenspan, *The Age of Turbulence*, The Penguin Press, New York, N.Y., 1970, pg. 306 & 309

5. Martin Feldstein, *A National Bureau of Economic Research Council*, University of Chicago Press, 1988

6. "Consumer Confidence Index", *Wikipedia, the Free Encyclopedia*, 2011, pg. 1

7. "Price/Earnings Ratio", *Wikipedia, the free encyclopedia*, 2011

8. "Fiscal Policy", *Wikipedia, the Free Encyclopedia*, 2011

9. "United States Federal Budget", *Wikipedia, the Free Encyclopedia*, 2011, pg. 5

10. IBID.

11. IBID

12. "United States Public Debt", *Wikipedia, the Free Encyclopedia*, 2011

13. "Monetary Policy", *Wikipedia, the Free Encyclopedia*, 2011

14. "401(k)", *Wikipedia, the Free Encyclopedia*, 2011

15. "Annuities" *U.S. Securities and Exchange Commission*

16. "Annuity (U.S. financial products)", *Wikipedia, the Free Encyclopedia*, 2011

17. "Derivatives (Finance)", *Wikipedia, the Free Encyclopedia*, 2011, pg. 7

18. IBID, pg. 2

19. "Hedging" *Columbia Encyclopedia*, pg. 1

20. "Futures contract," *Wikipedia, the Free Encyclopedia*, pg. 1

21. "Option (Finance)", *Wikipedia, the Free encyclopedia,*, pg. 1

22. "Credit Default Swap," *Wikipedia, the Free Encyclopedia*, pg. 1

23. "Derivatives," *The Economist*, March 5th 2011, pg. 81

24. *Bloomberg Business Week Magazine*, 12/5/2010, pg. 36

25. "Financial Crisis (2007 - present)" *Wikipedia, the Free Encyclopedia*, 2011, pg 1.

26. IBID, pg. 8

27. IBID, pg.11.

28. IBID, pg. 12

29. IBID, pg. 14
30. IBID, pg.18.
31. IBID. pg 18.
32. IBID, pg. 19
33. IBID, pg. 19
34. IBID, pg. 19
35. IBID, pg. 20
36. IBID, pg 23

www.ingramcontent.com/pod-product-compliance
Lightning Source LLC
Chambersburg PA
CBHW022104170526
45157CB00004B/1480